Tie Me Up!

For fifteen years now, alternative health practitioner **Stefan Niederwieser** has delighted his readers with both his moving stories of love and relationships and his entertaining guidebooks (among them, the bestseller *Bend Over! The Complete Guide to Anal Sex*). He also writes erotica under the pseudonym Gerke van Leiden.

After several long periods of time spent in the United States, the Bavarian-born writer chose Berlin as the setting where he and his husband now enjoy their conjugal bliss.

Aside from sex and writing, his reigning passion is *multi-generational trauma therapy*. For more on the author and his practice, see www.stephan-niederwieser.de

Stephan Niederwieser

TIE ME UP!

The Complete Guide to Bondage

BRUNO GMÜNDER

Tie Me Up!

1st Edition 2013
Copyright © 2013 Bruno Gmünder Verlag GmbH, Germany
Original title: Bondage-Fibel. Eine fesselnde Einführung
Text: © Stephan Niederwieser
Translation: Nicola Heine
Cover photo: © VanDarkholme.com
Back cover photo: © BoundJocks.com
Photo credits: page 202

Bruno Gmünder Verlag GmbH
Kleiststraße 23-26, 10787 Berlin
info@brunogmuender.com

Printed in Germany

ISBN 978-3-86787-599-8

More about Bruno Gmünder books and authors:
www.brunogmuender.com

His feet and then his hands, she together bound them all,
To a nail she carried him and hung him on the wall.

Description of Brunhild and Gunther's wedding night
from the *Nibelungenlied*, ca. 1200

Please note:

Ropes don't have a mind of their own. As a rule, a tied-up person is often unable or else lacks the skills to decide what is right and what is wrong, what is dangerous and what is safe, what gives him pleasure and what makes him panic. Therefore, the responsibility for rope play, for everything that happens during bondage and for all the consequences that may follow, lies with the person tying him up. Before you go ahead and start tying yourself or another person up with ropes, please read the safety tips at the end of the book. If there is anything you don't understand or if you're not sure, please consult an experienced practitioner before you endanger yourself and others.

All the knots and techniques described in this book have been tested to the best of our knowledge. The publishers and the author assume no liability for any damage or injuries caused by emulating them.

I would like to thank the photo model Felix Barca, who let himself be tied up (and tortured) by Master Bernd for hours during our photo shoot, Lars for the long balls, and Mischa for the photos, the studio, and the great atmosphere while we were shooting.

What's Inside

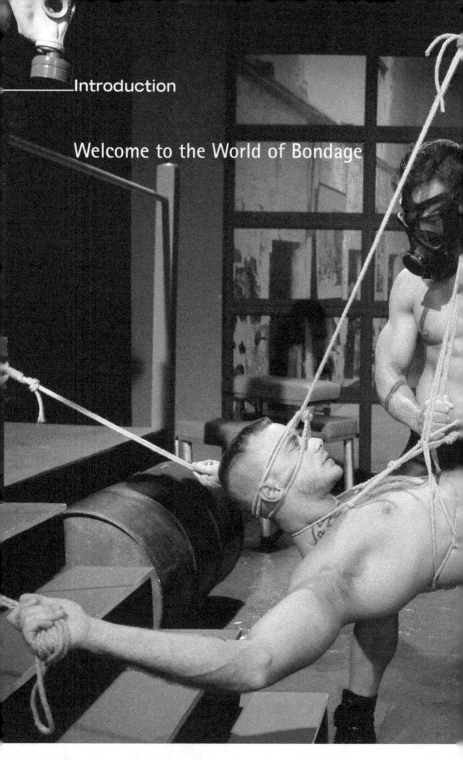

Welcome to the World of Bondage

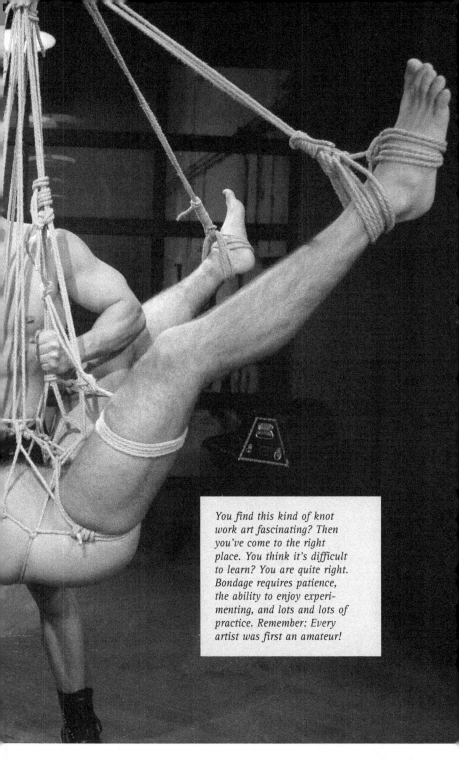

You find this kind of knot work art fascinating? Then you've come to the right place. You think it's difficult to learn? You are quite right. Bondage requires patience, the ability to enjoy experimenting, and lots and lots of practice. Remember: Every artist was first an amateur!

Keeping It Simple

Before breaking out the heavy ropes and the complicated
knots, you might want to try a preliminary taste of the thrill
of tying and being tied, of being defenceless, or of having
power over someone, the thrill of surprise, anticipation,
or even fear.

*Blindfolds: Fetter your senses and unfetter your imagination.
Being unable to see what's coming (in every conceivable
sense of the word) will increase your anticipation.*

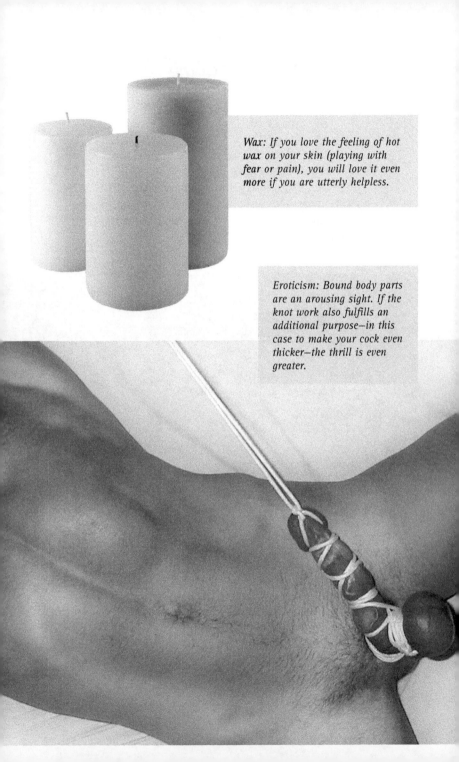

Wax: If you love the feeling of hot wax on your skin (playing with fear or pain), you will love it even more if you are utterly helpless.

Eroticism: Bound body parts are an arousing sight. If the knot work also fulfills an additional purpose—in this case to make your cock even thicker—the thrill is even greater.

Suspension: The art of the "rope dance," tying somebody up and suspending them bodily in midair.

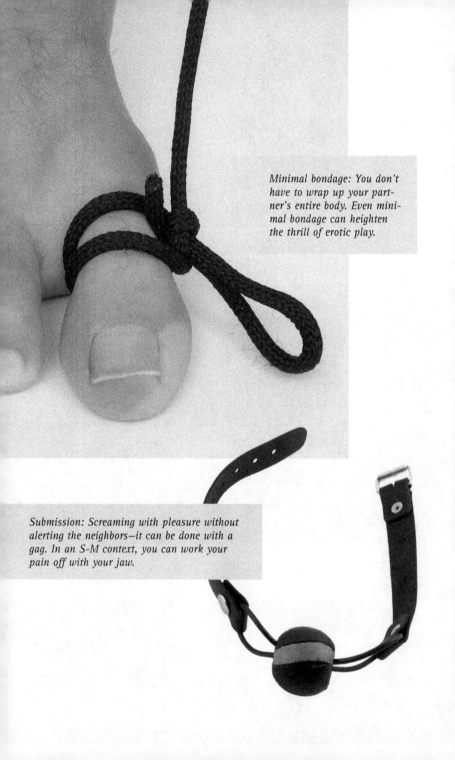

Minimal bondage: You don't have to wrap up your partner's entire body. Even minimal bondage can heighten the thrill of erotic play.

Submission: Screaming with pleasure without alerting the neighbors—it can be done with a gag. In an S-M context, you can work your pain off with your jaw.

S-M: And of course, bondage can serve as a wonderful basis for all kinds of S-M play.

Closeness: Playing with the physical proximity and distance between top and bottom can also transform your bondage experience.

Playing for time: Using devices that can be programmed to open after a fixed period of time, practitioners of self-bondage can place themselves at the mercy of an object.

Aesthetics: The sheer perfection of the knot work will set your heart racing.

Hands behind his head and completely immobilized. What for?
Sex, for instance.

Types of Bondage: An Overview

**"Latex, rubber jacket, rings of steel—
How far can I go?
Ecstasy in black, candle wax, stiletto heels –
I want to watch you!
Defenceless passion, shining leather, corsets of steel –
Helpless and beautiful!"**

From the song "Mondo Bondage" by Die Ärzte, from the album
Runter mit den Spendierhosen, 2000.

▼ Bondage and Passion—An Isolated Phenomenon?

By no means. Unfortunately I have no current date to back this statement up with, but an Internet search will yield studies showing that 24% of those American students surveyed entertained bondage fantasies during sex, while among homo- and bisexual men, the number was as high as 40%. As many as 34% of gay men have had some bondage experience. A survey on JoyClub.de concluded that 73% of their 5,000 (!) users had occasionally tried out this form of erotic play.

At the top of the list of bondage toys are handcuffs, used by 55% of the players (particularly the younger crowd), while 48% enjoy rope bondage and 33% use silk restraints.

So, you are by no means alone. Although the topic might raise a few eyebrows down in the bible belt or your parish church, it is generally safe to discuss these kinds of fantasies and practices in most major cities. Practically everyone will know what the term "bondage" means.

▼ Japanese Art?

The origins of this sexual practice—as of many other sexual topics—have been the subject of much speculation. But one thing is certain—at some point, the Japanese were involved. There are a number of techniques that were originally used to punish criminals or to torture enemy combatants (Kinbaku, Hojojutsu, Ninjitsu).

Bondage is also said to have been used in medieval Japan as a meditation aid. By binding and releasing one another, both partners were able to maintain a meditative state, similar to that achieved by raking a stone garden, or through archery, calligraphy, or tea ceremonies. Bondage means becoming one with the rope, mastering knots that have been handed down for centuries, and can help one overcome one's ego and resolve into a sort of Nirvana (enlightenment).

Ah yes, the Japanese. There is a very fitting saying that goes a long way to explaining the Japanese fetish for meditative practices: "God was gracious to the Japanese, he gave them no natural resources."

PS: We won't get as far as enlightenment in this book. If you have successfully mastered the most important knots by the end of it, I will be perfectly content.

Top and Bottom

For the sake of simplicity, I will be using the classic terms "top" for the person doing the tying and "bottom" for the person being tied. I most decidedly do not want to suggest that the bottom is purely passive, which is what many people assume. You will come to see just how active the bottom is and how utterly at his mercy the top can be.

▼ The Fetters of Freedom

There are many reasons for letting yourself be tied up. One case in point is that you may experience a sort of masochistic pleasure in being unable to move, a type of suffering, pain, an inner torment that can be increased by struggling against the bonds and against the restraints. Others may, in turn, reach a state of inner freedom induced by the exterior immobilization, a state comparable to meditative states of consciousness. Imagine being suspended by ropes in midair, being able to let go of everything, without even having to contend with gravity, which is what we must do every day whenever we sit, stand, or walk. This enables us to feel the deep-seated tension within our bodies we are ordinarily not aware of. Letting go of this can even have a profound effect on the psyche. One may feel more accepted than in other situations; the special attention that the top pays in tying the knots may be interpreted as being taken care of, as being the focus, as a state of I-am-the-most-important-person-at-this-moment-in-time.

And of course, letting oneself be tied up is always an act of submission: I give up power, I give up self-determination, I give up control ... and entrust all of this to my partner. If he handles it with care and responsibility, this can intensify the emotional bond between both partners.

It's interesting that the name chosen for this technique is bondage, from the verb "to bond." This offers up a wide range of metaphors: Bondage means that we form a bond or a tie with another person. The rope serves as a substitute for the umbilical cord. One is bound, as in spellbound, captivated, aroused.

▼ The Art of Binding

According to a Swedish survey taken in 1995, 88% of gay men take the passive role during bondage play, which means that only 12% take the active role. But this also has its own attraction. The aesthetic pleasure in particular lies with the top, after all, he is the one who, with the aid of a couple of ropes, transforms the body of the person at his mercy, into a work of art, which he can then contemplate and enjoy at his own leisure. But most tops are generally more interested in the power dynamic that develops during play. Not least, bondage also serves to keep the bottom submissive while one pounces on him during S-M play.

▼ Many Roads Lead Away from Rome

But there are a number of other motivations worth following up on in familiarizing oneself with bondage techniques. In the following, I will only be briefly alluding to them, so that you can let them inspire you to understand your own enjoyment of this form of interpersonal communication. Sooner or later you will be master of your *own*, special form of bondage.

▶ **Trying out something new:** It doesn't always have to be oral or anal sex—you should never neglect your sex life, especially with a

Couples bondage: Get your sex life off the beaten path.

partner. There is no better antidote to boredom than trying out something new. Tying your partner up or being tied up is one thing, but the game needn't stop here. Try pulling the ropes, pushing, squeezing, rolling, pinching, stroking …

▶ **Tension or fear orgasms:** Some people have to overcome an enormous barrier of fear in order to be able to give up control. This alone can lead to so much emotional tension that it may result in orgasm—without laying a finger on anyone.

▶ **As therapy:** In the hands of an experienced therapist, bondage can also take on aspects of self-awareness or even healing. My friend Jorgos even ties up his partners in order to clarify the dynamics of their partnership by this method. How does this work? You simply tie up your partner—in every sense of the word. What happens when my husband and I are tied together? Does this cause anxiety? Am

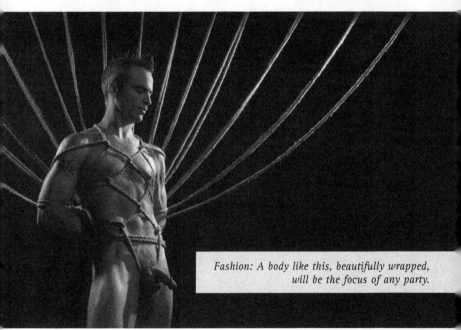

Fashion: A body like this, beautifully wrapped, will be the focus of any party.

Artwork by the American fetish king, Rick Castro, Los Angeles

I able to enjoy it? An attentive therapist can, in addition, steer the impulses of the persons involved, inhibiting or intensifying them by pulling the ropes.

▶ **Art:** Artistic ropework onstage is frequent sight. Opera houses in particular love to make the headlines time and again by employing these techniques to "*epater la bourgeoisie*".

But some sophisticated suspensions, set in motion and then filmed, are works of art themselves. The artist can also incorporate himself into the artwork, which then becomes a performance.

▶ **Fashion:** I don't think I have to do much explaining here. Without having verified it, I assume that these days even the designers for fashion catalogues have borrowed elements from the bondage scene.

▶ **Power play:** This always sounds as if the bottom gives up all control. But that doesn't necessarily have to move in one direction only. The bottom could just as easily tie up the top and determine how he wants to be fucked.

▶ **Unfamiliar experiences:** In a suspension, you are tied up (not free), while enjoying the feeling of floating in midair (freedom). Those with an esoteric bent would probably point to the connection "upstairs," but feel free to interpret this as you see fit.

▶ **Beautiful scars:** It may seem unusual to you, but some people really appreciate the rope marks, or "scars" left on the body by hard bondage. Go figure.

▶ **Accentuating the positive:** You can also use knots to emphasize particular bodily features, for example, the nipples, cock, or balls, to great effect. Additionally, tying these body parts off makes them more sensitive to stimuli.

▶ **S-M:** Tying someone up or being tied are of course key elements of S-M play. If you are interested but don't think you'd be a good slave, remember this maxim: "There are no bad slaves, only bad masters."

▶ **Accupressure:** A friend of mine once told me about a dom who was able to manipulate meridian points with knotted ropes, thereby performing a type of accupressure. I have unfortunately never been able to experience this myself. But I'll admit, I'm curious.

▶ **Bondage as metaphor:** The exceptional artist Michael Kirwan once wrote to me (in a review of my novel *On a Wednesday in September*), stating that in his opinion, gay men are such keen practitioners of bondage because the ropes can help externalize what they feel inside, that they are bound by societal and religious conventions. In this sense (and this would be a psychological interpretation), materializing this feeling of being tied up can be a way of becoming aware of yourself, of how you really feel, and can actually be liberating.

▶ **Postural defects:** This is just hearsay, but bondage was allegedly used in ancient China in order to correct postural problems, whereas in this country we need elaborate, custom-made corsets.

▶ **Massage:** Bondage can be a form of massage or "tied in" within a massage context.

▶ **Communication:** When couples play, they can use the rope or ropes to communicate who they are to their partners.

▶ **Captivity:** You can also tie someone up if you don't want to give him up. (Just kidding!)

▼ Rough as a Cowboy

As you can see, I often emphasize the psychological aspects of bondage. I firmly believe that bondage is the sexual practice with the greatest influence on the mind. It is therefore no doubt helpful if you come to an agreement with your partner on what you want the bondage to achieve bondage before you start.

What is even more important, in my opinion, is to agree on the type of bondage. When tying someone up, you can do this with the technical perfection of an architect or the sloppiness of an underpaid construction worker. You can be as painstakingly careful as a mountaineer about to climb Mount Everest, securing himself against a deadly fall, or virile and rough as a cowboy tying up a wildly struggling calf about to be branded. Others may wish to create award-winning macramé. As a top, you can manhandle the bottom, tugging and pushing at him, as a master would expect to treat a disobedient slave. But then you might proceed as slowly and sensuously as a Tantric master, stroking him, shaking the rope near his ear so that he can hear it, holding it under his nose to let him smell it, slowly drawing it across his skin ...

▼ Other Ways of Doing It

In brief: slow vs. fast, or rather, making unpredictable changes between the two. Following a previous agreement or explaining every step in detail, like a dentist about to drill your teeth. Or simply taking him completely by surprise (having agreed upon this beforehand). With or without talking. A suspended person can be left in situ or you can constantly change his position. You can keep your distance physically or you can accompany his movements. All of this can be done naked, clothed, or dressed up in fetish wear. You can recreate positions from books, as a pianist recreates the works of great composers, or you can venture upon your own visual melody, which might then inspire others. You can fit a finished creation onto your partner or you can adjust the knots to fit him. There is elaborate bondage and very simple bondage. And if you are used to "working" in the light, try moving to a twilight setting or to pitch darkness

Make the knot work beautiful and the rest will follow.

illuminated only by a headlamp, like the ones used by miners at the coalface. That way, the top can see parts of the bottom, but the bottom can hardly see the top. And last but not least, you can also incorporate other equipment (bars, chairs, crosses) into the setting, or work in free-form mode. On the floor. Standing up. Statically or in continual motion ...

The Right Type of Bondage

As you can see, there are a number of "reasons" you might want to tie someone up or be tied. Likewise, you can integrate bondage into sex play in a number of ways. S-M is only one option among many others. In this book I won't focus on a certain type of bondage, but rather concentrate on teaching you the basics, how to make knots in a rope in order to safely restrain someone's physical freedom of movement. I will leave whichever road you choose to lead you away from Rome up to your own curiosity and playfulness.

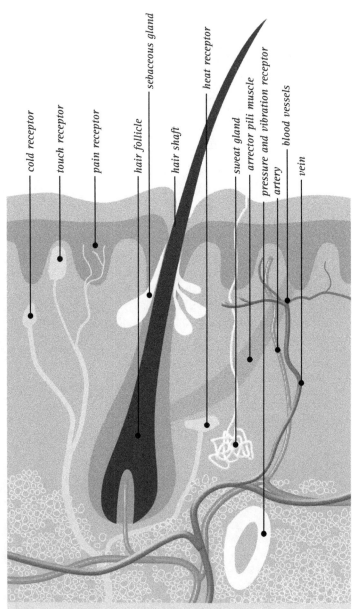

cold receptor
touch receptor
pain receptor
hair follicle
sebaceous gland
hair shaft
heat receptor
sweat gland
arrector pili muscle
pressure and vibration receptor
artery
blood vessels
vein

Cross section of skin with nerves and blood vessels

What You Definitely Need to Know

As exciting as bondage is, this practice does harbor certain risks. A brief introduction to the anatomy of the human body and the way of the rope will help you to avoid them. An overview of the most important basics.

In the same way as knowing a bit about the structure of the intestines will help you reach your goal when fisting (!), and knowing how internal organs react to blows is essential before you start flogging anyone as part of S-M play, you should also try to recall a few facts about the anatomy of the human body you learned about in biology class before you start applying your ropes to another person's extremities. To avoid causing damage to yourself or your playmate, it is also helpful to take into account a couple of points about the workings of the mind.

▼ Circulation
In order to function properly, the human body, every nook and cranny, every last cell of it, needs a constant supply of blood. And the reason we can move our muscles, feel (heat, cold, pressure, friction), or grow goose bumps—which can look so enchanting during erotic play—is because our skin is criss-crossed with a network of nerve cells.

Light pressure, as for instance caused by the tight cuffs of a pullover, presents no problem. However, if the body is subjected to sudden heavy pressure (impact), if the pressure is so great as to strongly inhibit blood supply to the region (knots placed over main blood vessels), this can lead to hematoma (bruising), swelling (caused by fluid congestion) or even numbness (when a limb "goes to sleep").

Within S-M play, certain techniques are used to deliberately elicit these reactions. In bondage without S-M, you can also let the bottom experience these sensory stimuli (this must always be closely monitored in order to avoid long term damage). A simple bondage session, one followed by sexual intercourse, does not need to go beyond gentle pressure.

Pay special attention to those places where you can feel a pulse: on the wrists, knees, armpits, and of course the neck (carotid arteries). Never tie the knots too tightly and always keep the lines of communication with the bottom open to check whether he is comfortable (if you've gagged him, use eye contact! If that, too, is impossible, use a safety signal. See also our chapter on *Safety Measures*).

You are presumably aware of the fact that joints can and should only be stretched to a certain extent. But please don't forget that some people are less flexible than others and that overstraining can lead to cramps—which is no fun at all, especially if your limbs are tied.

▼ The Marks of Passion

Ropes leave marks on your skin. Depending on how tightly you have trussed up the bottom (or how tightly you've let yourself be tied), the ropes will dig into his or your skin. This is another thing to be aware of.

Ordinary bondage marks will generally fade after a quarter to half an hour, but the marks left by more tighter knots may be visible for a longer time. Rope burn (see "A Guide to Knots") not only hurts, it will also form a scab.

▼ Internal Organs

It is just as important to be aware of the location of particularly sensitive organs. Many people's necks are not even strong enough to carry the weight of their heads (as evinced by all the crooked backs you see around you), to say nothing of suspending an entire body from them without causing injury. And the torso is full of vital organs, connected to all sorts of blood vessels. You might be able to constrict these with a corset, if at all, but even that is rarely pleasant and can lead to fainting—just ask the ladies of bygone times, governed as they were by quite different ideals of slimness. It is extremely dangerous to try to constrict the torso with one rope, for example, by suspending it.

▼ Circulation
As a top, part of your responsibility consists of not losing sight of the bottom in his entirety (instead of just concentrating on his dick). Part of this involves keeping an eye on his pulse. If his heart suddenly starts to race or even stops, his blood pressure will drop (and the bottom will pass out) and the muscles will go slack. If he is standing upright at the time, then he will fall over (and hurt himself!). There are warning signs for this sort of thing: compulsive yawning (which you should not interpret as a sign of your inability to stage an exciting session), nausea, or feelings of dizziness. If he breaks out into a sweat, it is already too late. The only thing you can do is ...

Emergency Procedures
If the bottom feels sick or dizzy, quickly and carefully lay him down on his back, undo all the ropes immediately, raise his legs and stay calm. For additional measures, see *Safety Measures* page 196.

▼ Prevention
Yes, you can do that too. Many people forget how strenuous these sessions are. Even if it looks quite pleasant physically, being tied up can be an enormous psychological strain.

Especially when practicing in a warm space—which is generally a good idea if you're having a naked session—you should always have something to drink within easy reach. Dehydration is a drain on the circulatory system. During longer sessions, your blood sugar levels may drop, so keep some glucose tablets on hand!

▼ Nutrition

Inquire about any health issues your partner might have beforehand. If your slave is in HIV therapy, you won't want to lock him in the cellar for a week on a diet of bread and water, but rather make sure he can take his medications at the prescribed times.

For diabetics, or people with heart or blood pressure problems, taking their medications regularly is even more important, as they have not only the long-term consequences to deal with, but may also pass out on the spot. And then you'd be in a pretty pickle.

Adam's Apple

One body part which we rarely pay much attention to in everyday life is the Adam's apple, that weird bit of cartilage in your throat that moves up and down when you swallow and helps us tell men and women apart. And there's your problem right there. Ties around the neck (cervical collars, hangman's nooses, dog collars) are not for the inexperienced in any case, not matter how hot they may look or what your erotic associations with them may be. Should you prefer to disregard this warning, at least make sure that the noose is large enough for the Adam's apple to move up and down unscathed, as otherwise you may cause—relatively harmless—grazing or worse, panic.

▼ Establish a Safe Word

Anyone wearing a gag should be able to tell you in time if it's getting too much for him or if he feels nauseous or dizzy. To be on the safe side, you can have the bottom hold a couple of coins that will clink if he lets them drop. On a carpeted floor you can use small metal plates (novelty items that imitate the sound of breaking glass, available from novelty stores). Of course, all of this applies to you, too, if you wish to place yourself in someone else's hands.

▼ Erectile Tissue

If you tie off someone's dick, it will generally get harder and even a bit bigger. You'll be familiar with this effect from cock rings. But if you tie it too tightly, you can interrupt the blood supply or even injure the poor sensitive thing. Ever heard of penile fractures? Your schlong will first turn blue, and then black. Not a good look, not very healthy and no fun at all, especially if it grows back together all crooked (which can happen!).

▼ Psychological Aspects

One could say quite a lot about the role of the mind. Perhaps most importantly: Newcomers to the world of bondage will have no idea of what they are in for and how it will make them feel. They will only be equipped with a few fantasies and perhaps a couple of porn images, in which some random hardened and generally drugged up model undergoes all sorts of extreme treatment in order to finance

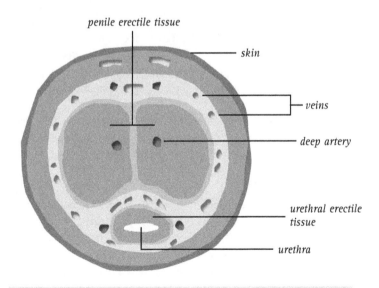

penile erectile tissue

skin

veins

deep artery

urethral erectile tissue

urethra

Cross section of the penis

his (mostly not that great) life by simulating passion for other people's benefit. With newbies, you should actually assume that they will tend to "bite off more than they can chew" (as they say). So don't take everything at face value.

Don't forget to always keep an eye on your partner. No matter how often he says, "That's hot, harder, tighter, deeper," if you can see the panic rising in his face, the sweat beading on his forehead even though it's not that warm, then take it down a notch. If he passes out, he might injure himself permanently, and then you'll be up to your neck in it.

And there is another thing that can happen to you (it happened to me): A beginner wanted to finally live out his fantasy. I tied him up and he went increasingly quiet on me, slowly but surely his facial expression changed from one of tense anticipation to pain. I checked in with him, he wanted more, clenching his teeth and squeezing his eyes shut. Suddenly he panicked and started thrashing about like a maniac. I undid the knots and he gradually calmed down. Later on, he told me that this scenario of being defenseless had triggered images inside him: As a child he had been tied to the bed and sexually abused by his grandfather. This memory had been buried deep inside his unconscious mind and had then been reenacted by the bondage experience.

Not everybody knows where the fantasies that dog their every step come from. For some, a desire can conceal split-off emotions whose origins lie in a trauma that they cannot (yet) remember.

▼ Know Thyself
If I've guessed right, then those small-scale wrist cuffs don't quite hold your attention as much as the sophisticated "artworks," men tied up outdoors, suspended naked between two trees like a fly in a spider web. It's a good thing to aim for, a good thing to want to be able to do just as well someday, but it's just as important to stay realistic.

What You Should Never Do

Never overstep a bottom's boundaries. His "stop!" means stop. Do not demand too much of him ("Oh, don't make such a fuss!"), never abuse your playmate's trust in you. Nor should you ever expect too much of him. And never forget to keep a sharp pair of scissors at hand in case you need to quickly cut through thick ropes (EMT shears).

This is how you can achieve your goal: You will quickly master the short preliminary exercises as described in this book and at some point you will feel you have enough experience to venture a suspension. You make your own elaborate harness and it looks really nice and fits beautifully. The bottom is already in a state of trance, then you hang him from the ceiling, pull him up with the rope ... and the whole damn thing slips. The bottom turns blue in the face, you open the panic snaps and carefully lower him back to the ground and back to life. Then you go to the bathroom and squirt a handful of shaving cream at your reflection in the mirror to cool down your frustration.

▼ It Happens to Everyone!

Hang in there! Don't give up! Bondage isn't a given, it has to be learned. That takes time. Don't ask too much of yourself! Don't let your expectations get too high! Proceed step by step. Start with suspending just one arm. Then a leg. Then a guy in a pelvic harness (if that slips, it at worst will be a bit painful), or a shoulder harness without (!!!) the neck loop. And preferably without tying his arms or legs so that he can assist you in an emergency.

But I'm getting ahead of myself. Here's one more important step:

▼ Think like a Rope

Ropes can be coiled and tied and knotted and threaded ... they don't have a mind of their own, nor do they think for themselves. Sooner or later it will happen to you: However smart the harness you invent, at some point the whole damn thing will slip. So, never be too confident. Always reckon on having forgotten something, having to stop suddenly and quickly release the bottom.

Grrr. Sometimes things don't work out quite the way you planned. But be patient!

An Overview of the Most Important Points

- **Most important word:** Professionals agree on a word to indicate that it's getting too much and the other person needs to stop right away. Internationally, the word "mayday" has become widely accepted for this purpose. I still prefer the traffic light colors, as they include not only "stop" (red) and "go" (green) but also an in-between, something like "we're getting close to my limits. From now on proceed with great care" (amber).

- **Most important relationship element:** power. No matter what type of bondage you choose and how you do it, in bondage play, the subject of power is inescapable. One person relinquishes it, the other takes it on. This does not however have to culminate in S-M play. The term "consensual" is often used here to show that one agrees upon the rules of play.

- **Most important knot:** none. You can wrap someone up properly without tying a single knot. But it's good to know some of them, see our chapter *A Guide to Knots*.

- **Most important utensil:** a pair of EMT shears you can use to quickly cut through the ropes.

- **Most imporant number:** 911 (this number will connect you with emergency medical services throughout the country).

- **Most important decision:** Do I trust my partner or not? If not, don't do it!

- **Most important feeling:** the willingness to give up control. This applies to both partners.

- **Most important skill:** empathy, being able to know what another person is feeling. In addition, it is helpful for a top if he has both stamina and willingness to learn, because only practice, practice and more practice makes perfect.

For some people, the sheer presence of ropes is orgasm-inducing.

Learning the Ropes

Tying a man up is a bit like building a house: If you've got the right tools, it's not only easier, you also get a nicer result.

Of course, if you have a number of specially designed and produced devices such as cuffs, bondage-wear, or straitjackets on hand, you can create very elaborate bondage scenarios. I'll go into this in more detail in *Tools and Aids* page 166. In this chapter we will be mainly looking at ties. Following a brief overview of different materials, I will be taking a closer look at ropes. For if you understand the art of ropemaking, you will be able to confidently and effortlessly create a magnificent work of bondage art—provided you're still even interested in working with anything but rope ...

▼ Metal

Chains rattle delightfully, they are sturdy (a not unimportant advantage, especially for suspensions), and in addition, their inflexibility serves as a metaphor no S-M practitioner would want to deny himself. This is why metal (generally stainless steel) is often used in bondage: manacles, shackles, thumb cuffs, hooks (with a ball attached at one end which can be inserted into various bodily orifices ...) and of course, chains, which can be used in combination with other tools to immobilize someone. In BDSM stories and comics, chains are frequently associated with historical torture or prison scenarios.

Chains

If applied directly to the skin, these materials can leave distinct pressure marks and their inflexibility means that the greatest care should be taken if you are using them around joints or for longer periods of time. (Be sure to file off the welding seams beforehand! Or else use professional gear.) Oh, and please don't use chains with open links, as these could bend open under strain. These should always be welded closed for safety's sake!

▼ Leather, Latex, and Rubber

Its strength and pliability make leather an equally popular material in bondage. Besides which, it can fulfill a number of fetish fantasies: Some people refer to leather as a second skin, they see an animal's skin as being erotically (animalistically) charged.

Easy to take care of and to work with, leather is also commonly used for homemade bondage equipment. Ready-made bondage aids (cuffs, body bags, bodies) are often made of leather. See our chapter on *Tools and Aids*.

▼ Other Materials

Some other materials are foils and wraps or tape, either bondage tape specially made for this purpose or those exercise bands used in gymnastics (just borrow them from your grandma!). Another member of this group in the widest sense is plastic wrap, which can be used for purposes other than the one its creator intended, for instance mummification or Saran Wrap bondage—not quite the same as keeping things fresh.

Materials such as self-adhesive and other bandages are generally used only within a sort of general medical fetish scenario. Other rarely used materials with medical associations are plaster bandages.

Things can get even more exotic: One photographer tied his models up with LED strips and captured their images in total darkness, so that only the outlines and certain parts of their bodies were visible. Very nice.

The more romantic souls among us may prefer their presents wrapped in satin bows. Silk scarves are also popular, preferably by Hermès ... (I'm being a bit snarky here). But I really shouldn't make fun of these practices. After all, my first bondage experiences began with a silk tie. What was so great about that? I haven't the slightest notion, it wasn't my idea.

And while we're at it, of course you can use a scarf. I don't mean that as a dig against the eco-freaks, just pointing out that sometimes you've got to work with what's on hand. Winter ... park ... got it?

Last but not least, I would like to draw your attention to shoelaces. Not as suitable for tying up large limbs or more sensitive members, but well suited to tying up fingers. Of course, only when you are not planning on encountering any resistance from the bottom.

Hang on, have I mentioned cable ties yet?

Unusual Alternatives to Ropes

Round cord profiles. You can get them in dark grey, with a 12 mm diameter. Originally developed to insulate steel frames, they are typically used for front and interior door-frames. Which brings us back to: working with what you've got ... by the way, they are made of TPE (thermoplastic elastomer), which is highly weatherproof, heat resistant from -76 to 212 degrees Fahrenheit, and resistant to light, tearing, UV rays, and ozone. If you have enough time on your hands, you can paint the profiles using water soluble acrylics or any other eco-friendly paints. A note to all our eco-conscious friends: this product is 100% recyclable. And incidentally, it fits sleekly around your bones and skin.

▼ Ropes

After our brief excursion into the world of alternatives, we now come to the matter in hand: In general, ropes are the medium of choice for physical bondage. In Western bondage, almost all types of rope materials are used, among them cotton, synthetic fibers, or mixed materials. By contrast, Shibari (Japanese bondage) materials are limited to ropes made almost exclusively out of hemp and jute.

These materials are often treated before use to make them as soft and supple as possible and to ensure that they smell nice. See below for more. Pre-treating the ropes has become less popular of late.

▼ Types, Qualities, and Colors

Quite a variety of ropes can be used for bondage, among these sisal, jute, hemp, Japanese hemp, cotton, nylon, and other synthetics. Don't ask which is best. It's a bit like different cities. A New Yorker would never go to a Midwestern restaurant, Floridians cannot imagine living in Portland, and Texans are born and die in the Lone Star State. Each material has its own advantages and disadvantages, especially with regard to hygiene and cleaning. There are differences in not only odor and texture, but also in color and flexibility. In addition, every material leaves different marks on your skin ... Not least of all, you should be clear about your own hygienic expectations.

It is of course a good idea to consult an expert, but in the end you will just hear the same thing you would at a fetish consultation: What do you want? As you presumably don't and can't know that yet, I would suggest you pick up different types of ropes, touch them, sniff at them, draw them across your skin and (if no one's watching), put them in your mouth and taste them. Bondage is above all a sensual experience. That is why all your senses should be aroused, otherwise there's not much point to all of it. You can compare bondage to gift-wrapping: Do you want the ribbon to match the present? Or doesn't it matter?

▼ Cotton

Let's start with the more common materials. Cotton is very kind to the skin and doesn't cause rope burn that easily. Washing it will make it softer and you can also dye it. Those are the advantages. On the other hand, it will fray (not just at the ends!) and soil easily, and moisture will harden it, which is why cotton is not well suited for sweaty athletic contests. Or for water sports or bathtub sessions, as it can be quite difficult to untie the knots again in a hurry ... If stored wet, cotton will go moldy and start to smell. In addition, it tends to expand and tears more easily than other materials.

And another thing: If you use coreless cotton ropes, the knots will tighten. Knots made with ropes that have a core are easier to untie.

Washing cotton will also make it tougher and less liable to tear if used in suspensions.

▼ Hemp

Hemp's natural warm golden color darkens with time (whether you treat it or not). You can also dye it, but even left in its natural state, its color makes it a lovely sight to behold when placed on your skin.

Hemp smells of grass or hay (unless you treat it with strong smelling oils), hardly expands at all, and can therefore take the strain of any type of knot. If pre-treated properly, it will not leave rope burns on your skin. (But it will if you don't treat it.) See below for how to care for hemp ropes.

Hemp

Being a natural material, hemp comes in a wide variety of qualities, depending on your source. But even hemp made by the same rope maker may vary in quality. It is also sold under different names. Western hemp is heavier and more tightly coiled, Japanese hemp is lighter and silkier. You can also get braided hemp, but that is more difficult to knot and will not be kind to your skin.

You can test its strength by uncoiling the rope (turn the ends against one another!). If it uncoils easily, then it's loosely coiled, which makes it easier to use but also means that it won't be very stable and will fray easily (if you apply a lot of friction). It will also fall apart more readily if you machine-wash it a lot. If you have to exert a lot of strength to uncoil your rope, that means it's firmer and more resilient, but also more difficult to knot. As you see, there's a catch to everything.

▼ Jute

Another natural fiber, jute generally smells sweeter than hemp, but is otherwise very similar in resilience, pliability and the way it feels on your skin. As with hemp, jute should be pre-treated before use. When knotting, it tends to sound crunchy, which some people enjoy.

Oh, and one disadvantage: It expands quite a lot, especially when wet, so it's not really suitable for aquatic bondage.

▼ Nylon

No question, synthetic fibers are cheapest. They also have a smooth silky surface which feels pleasant on your skin. They rarely burn your skin and their flexibility makes knotting easy. They also don't expand much (as compared to, say, cotton). But nor do they hold knots very well. If you don't want your partner to escape, you may have to add an extra knot here and there.

Dyeing nylon is a bit difficult, but nylon ropes are available in all sorts of colors. There are waterproof and therefore easy to clean, which makes them the best option for anything involving water or lots of sweaty action.

▼ Climbing Ropes

These especially resilient synthetic fibers will feel quite hard on your skin and burn you easily. Apart from that, climbing ropes are very stiff and difficult to work with. But they're great for suspensions. Expensive though ...

▼ Washing Lines

While inexpensive, washing lines are very stubborn and difficult to bend, even if you heat them. They are also too thin and hard for many knots. On the other hand, they are weatherproof, in case you plan on tying your slave to a tree in the snow and the rain, but ... oh, just forget it, ok?

▼ Others

Anyone who has set foot in a well stocked hardware or possibly even a boating supply store will know that there are countless other fibers to be had: coconut fiber, bungee cords, parachute cords, polyester, polypropylene, viscose, rubber tubing, sisal, anchor or towing ropes. As I said, go take a look and cop a feel.

▼ Yes, but ...

Supposing I like hemp but my bottom prefers cotton? Well, you're going to have to come to an agreement. In my humble opinion, shady compromises are rarely much help. If nylon isn't your thing but your bottom insists on it, you won't have much fun, and if you don't have fun, neither will he. A better solution: a different partner.

▼ Length and Thickness

Start out with 6-8 mm and use your common sense. You'll need thicker ropes for suspensions. You can also use

Nylon

Washing lines

Other Ropes

thicker ropes to tie extremities. Naturally, you'll only want 3-4 mm for ball or finger bondage.

"Double rope technicians" please remember: six millimeters doubled up are twelve millimeters!

For genital bondage a 2.5 meter long rope should suffice. A nice and complex chest harness may eat up as much as 25 meters. But there's not much point in using ropes that long, as you have to keep pulling the whole length through the loop. Limit yourself to 8 to 10 meters. I'll explain later on how to join them.

Rope Burn
Pulling a rope tightly and quickly across skin will cause chafing. How easily your skin can be torn by the rope depends on the material (see above). The best way to prevent rope burns is to always pull the rope across your fingers and not tightly over the bottom's skin. Take note: the more slowly you pull, the less the danger of rope burn.

▼ Treatment
Hemp is sold untreated. It is very rough, contains husks and the weave can be—depending on quality—irregular. In its pure state, it might tempt a masochist at best, but most people won't be up for treating skin abrasions afterwards.

Treating your equipment yourself is admittedly a lot of work, but it will help you "bond" with your ropes. Cut the rope to the desired length. Knot the ends to prevent them from fraying and then boil it for about an hour in a big pot. Stir occasionally. Then let it drain and cool off before you wring it out (or else you'll burn your fingers).

Another option is to machine wash it at 200° F. Laundry detergent will bleach your rope and chlorine will wear it out. Shampoo is a better option—but not too much, or your washing machine will suds up.

Whether you use a washing machine or a cooking pot will depend on the quality of your rope. A loosely coiled rope in the washing machine will be turned to mush.

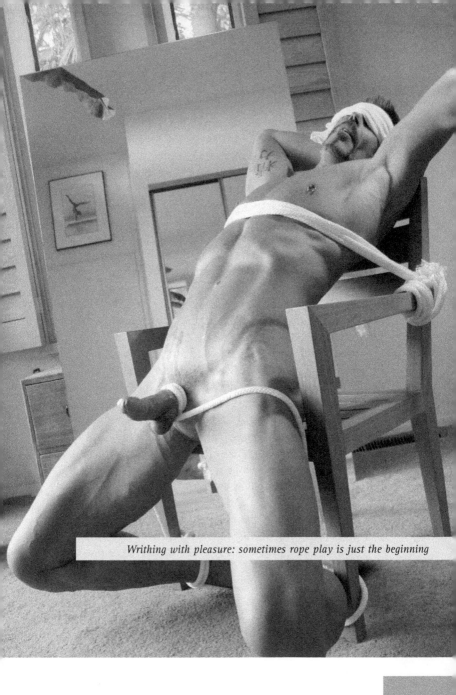

Writhing with pleasure: sometimes rope play is just the beginning

After you've let it drain and wrung it out, leave your rope out on top of a dryer for a couple of days. This will cause some shrinkage, so if you want to keep the original length, stretch it over a drying frame or wrap it tightly around a reel.

Next step: straightening. For this you will need an open flame. Use a candle for a more sedate pace or a camping stove for more speed and added danger. If you have nice roommates, you might want to turn it into an opportunity for a garden party, as this will take a while. Starting at one end, draw the rope over the flame while twisting it round. This will burn off the husks and rough bits (remove larger husks beforehand with tweezers!). It is important to singe the rope off at the right speed. Too fast and it will make your bottom scream later on. If it catches fire, then you've spent too long in one place.

Yes, it can get pretty boring, especially if you plan on preparing a number of ropes at once. But as I said before, turn the whole thing into a garden party, invite the neighbors over, and you'll be dining off of their reactions for months to come.

Finally, you'll need to remove all the charred bits. You can use an old rag soaked in hemp oil for this. I prefer fabric work gloves myself, because they won't slip off your fingers. Slowly draw the rope through from front to back and then back again. Make sure the oil is distributed evenly, so the rope isn't soaking wet in some places and bone-dry in others. Alternatives to hemp oil are leather grease, baby oil (smells terrible) or beeswax (smells delicious).

Before using, give the rope a good working over by pulling it through a hook in the ceiling several times. And there you go.

PS: You will find riggers who prefer to singe off the rope first and then wash it, to avoid having to remove the charred bits. That is an option. But if the husks swell up to the surface when you wash it, you will have to start over.

PPS: If you wash your ropes at your local laundromat, you'll have yourself a great conversation starter …

▼ How to Treat the Ends

If you ask an experienced rigger, they will tell you all sorts of ways of finishing rope ends. This is kind of a point of honor. I've noted a couple of options that made the most sense to me.

Burning the ends

▶ **Burning:** Synthetic fibers can be melted over a candle and smoothed down with a flat metal object. This is the simplest method. The ends will start to straggle after a while but that can be fixed easily.

▶ **Taping:** Cotton and hemp ropes can be wrapped with stong adhesive tape. This can look quite attractive if you put some effort into it. On the other hand, you will need to redo it every three washes or so.

Taping has the added advantage of letting you use different colored tape to help you tell your ropes apart; for example, as to length. They can also help you find your own ropes again amid the bustle of a bondage party (you can also use Band-Aid labels).

Taping the ends

▶ **Knotting:** The purists among us will use a simple knot to prevent their rope ends from fraying. This looks best. But the disadvantage is that these types of ends create a knob, which then has to be taken into account when tying up the bottom (especially when pulling the rope through a loop).

Knotting the ends

▼ Marking the Middle

When using longer ropes, it's a good idea to mark the middle with a narrow strip of tape. This is especially helpful for when you only have one hand free.

▼ Storage

At the risk of sounding like your mother, if you coil your ropes and store them properly, you save yourself a lot of fiddling around later on. Unpicking a nest of ropes is not generally considered the most erotic of foreplay.

▶ **Option 1:** Hold both ends in one hand and wrap the rope around your elbow and thumb. When there are only about 50 cm left, take hold of the coil, wind the rest around the middle, and pull the end through from underneath.

▶ **Option 2:** Takes longer, but works just as well: hold one end of the rope in your hand and wrap the rope around your elbow and

Your trusty retailer's great selection of ropes

your thumb, then wrap the other end around the middle and tie a knot.

However you do it, try and master one of the techniques. For it can get quite interesting if you have to coil your rope in the middle of a bondage session in order to tie it to your previous knots, but you only have one hand free because the other is holding the bottom ...

▼ Cleaning

If the only thing they've touched is skin, you won't need to wash your ropes. The oils and salts contained in sweat will actually make the material more supple. But if you get semen or blood on them, you will have to wash your ropes (unless you only play with one partner).

If blood gets on them (which can happen quicker than you'd think), soak the ropes in cold water right away. Then toss them straight in the washing machine and wash at 200°F. This will leave them visibly and hygienically clean.

Cleaning

Most materials can be machine washed (except for leather), but natural fibers will become brittle, hemp may uncoil, and cotton will start to unravel. Before washing it in a machine, I suggest you use a basic crochet technique to turn the rope into a loose chain and then stick it in a pillow slip before you put it in the machine. Otherwise your rope will tie itself in knots. If you boil it in a pot, just take care while stirring.

As long as you boil or wash at high temperatures, you won't need special cleaning solutions.

Sales Advice

I can only advise you to spare some consideration for the different materials yourself, as in the end it is really just a matter of taste.

It makes the most sense to ask at a sex shop where the owner knows a bit about bondage. Only they can really advise you. You don't really want to ask questions like "What kind of rope would you use to tie off someone's dick?" at a hardware store.

Sex shops have not been around for many years just because their salespeople look sexy, but because they can give their customers professional and competent advice.

Don't pinch pennies when you could be having so much more fun. In the final analysis, you will be paying more if you don't like the product. That's why I don't recommend online shopping in these cases, as you can't judge the quality until the amount has been deducted from your credit card ...

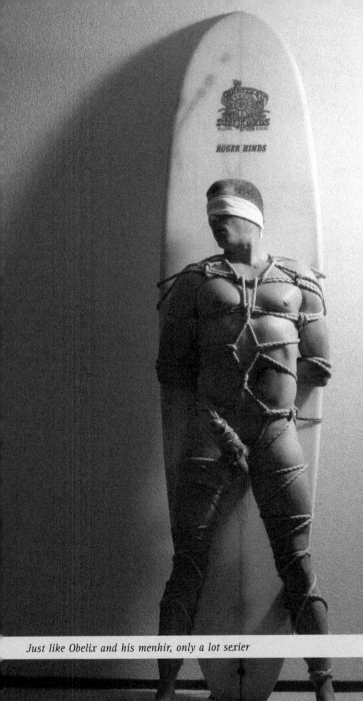

Just like Obelix and his menhir, only a lot sexier

Getting Knotty ...

Of course, the basis for rope bondage isn't just having the right ropes; knowing how to tie the right knots is also important. You will learn all you need to know here.

There are, of course, some riggers who will inform you that you can do bondage completely without knots. True. But this will pose some problems for a beginner, especially if they want to restrain their partners properly. Besides, it's never a bad thing to have some knots down pat. If you can then do without them, so much the better,

Incidentally, I have taken care to tie all the knots here very neatly. Just so you can tell from the photos how they are supposed to look. And well, personally I prefer an aesthetic look. But in no way do I mean to suggest that it is less arousing to tie your knots roughly, to be reduced to an animal state. As is generally known, personal tastes may differ.

PS: This chapter will let you practice on yourself so that you don't get on your sweetheart's nerves.

▼ Single / Double Rope Technique

Let's start with the basics, for which you don't even need to use a body. For example, the decision on whether to use a double or single

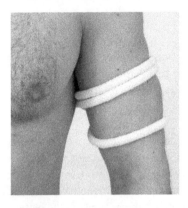

rope. Doubling up the rope will speed the whole procedure up (we want to savor it, but not at the expense of putting the bottom to sleep...), the loads are distributed more evenly (less fiddling) and it starts to look good sooner. Single rope techniques are best suited for delicate ropework, harnesses for instance, or genital bondage.

▼ Reef Knots

Two very important knots you should definitely know are the reef knot and Bernd's knot (the latter was named for our professional rigger who spent days patiently being photographed at work).

You will use reef knots most of all. This is because they are both secure and easy to untie. They are also incredibly easy to do. You will find Bernd's knot further down in the section *Single Limbs*.

1   lay the rope ends over one another (as if tying a shoelace)
2   cross them over again, but like this ...
3   then the end that was on top at first ...
4   is on top again. Tighten the knot and you're done!

A plain knot will open by itself if you pull on the rope. The brilliant part of the reef knot is that it gets tighter if you pull it. But it can still be easily untied: just push apart the loops you've made.

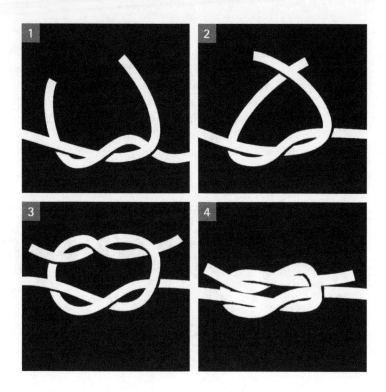

Where do knots come from?

You may want some conversation topics for longer sessions, so here's some information on the origin of the word *knot*: It has been around since the 8th century. From Old High German *knoto* or *knodo* (clearly a Japanese influence—just kidding!) via Middle High German *knode* or *knote*.

▼ Lark's Head or Cow Hitch

Use the cow hitch, for example, to incorporate spreader bars into bondage play. Or if you have attached cuffs to the bottom's limbs (see *Tools and Aids*) and would like to tie these to a rope.

1 Find the bight (the middle of the rope) and push it through the D-ring on the cuff or lay it around the bar.
2 Draw the open ends through the loop you've created and pull them tight. Done.

▼ Anchor Bend

If you've tied the bottom's joints with ropes and would like to tie the end to a St. Andrew's cross, for example, you will need another, more secure knot. The anchor bend is excellently suited to your needs:

1 Wrap one end around the bar twice.
2 Then pass the free end through both loops and under the bar.
3 Finally, secure the end with one or two half hitches.
4 Tighten the knot and you're done.

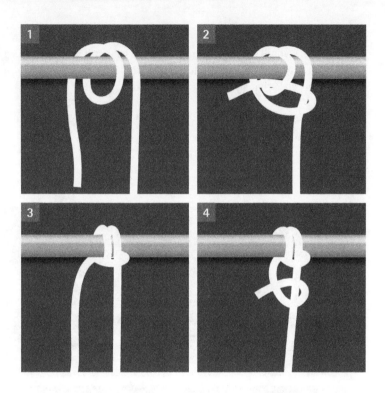

This knot is strong enough to hang a cow from (not that I'm encouraging you to have sex with animals), in case the rope isn't.

You and Your Knot
There are any number of knots and they all have their own advantages and disadvantages. You can go on and on learning. Remember, there are no right or wrong knots—unless you're competing in some kind of bondage contest. Tie them up, try them out, and someday, you'll find the knot that's right for you.

▼ Figure-Eight Knot

Sometimes you'll need to secure a rope end so that it won't be pulled through a loop. You can do this easily with a figure-eight knot, so called because that's just what it looks like.

1 Form a loop.
2 Pass the free end under the rope.
3 Then pass the end through the loop.
4 Pull it tight. Done.

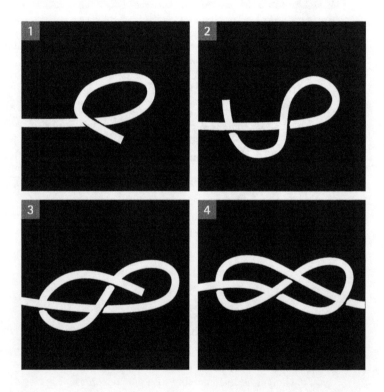

▼ Double Coin Knot

This is a rare but attractive knot. We stole it from the Two Knotty Boys, who call it the *double coin knot* because it looks a bit like two overlapping Chinese coins.

It may look complicated, but it's actually very simple. It's also very useful if you want to do more elaborate ropework. Examples given in this book are facial bondage and chest harnesses (fashion).

1 Practice by laying a short rope on the floor as pictured.
   Pay attention to where the loop is!
2 Now place the long end over the loop and under the short end.
3 All you have to do now is follow the rules for group sex: over and under, over and under ...
4 The long end goes over the first part of the large loop, then under the left side of the small one, over the right side of the large one and under the right side of the small one.
5 Pull it tight. Done!

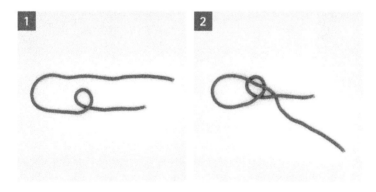

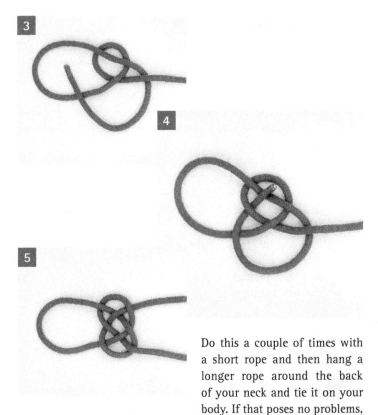

Do this a couple of times with a short rope and then hang a longer rope around the back of your neck and tie it on your body. If that poses no problems, then incorporate the knot into larger-scale bondage, for example, a crotch rope (see page 93). Once you're able to tie the double coin knot with your eyes closed, then you can try it out on someone else.

▼ Practice, Practice, and Practice Again

Once you have tied these knots a few times, try doing it with your eyes closed or in the dark. This will be a useful skill for when you start practicing in the depths of a darkroom.

Practicing untying knots in the dark is also not such a bad idea, in case some dreadful rigger decides to tie you up and leave you there. Just make like Houdini.

▼ Extending Your Rope (Joining)

If you're tying a harness or full-body bondage, you will have to extend your ropes at some point. There are several methods. For single rope techniques I would recommend the very attractive fisherman's knot. This is how you tie it:

1 Place the ropes parallel to one another, with the ends facing away from each other.
2 Tie each rope around the other in an overhand knot.
3 Pull them tight. Done!

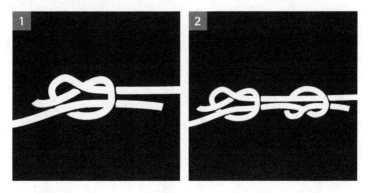

PS: If you're working with smooth synthetic fibers, tie each rope twice to make the knots more secure.

Other Alternatives

1 Find the bight, (the middle of the rope you want to extend) and wrap it around your fingers to create an empty lark's head.
2 Now pull the other rope through the loop.
3 Wrap one end once around the back of the rope ...
4 ... And pull it through the running loop from the other side ...
5 ... And then upwards through the other loop.
6 Pull it tight. Done!

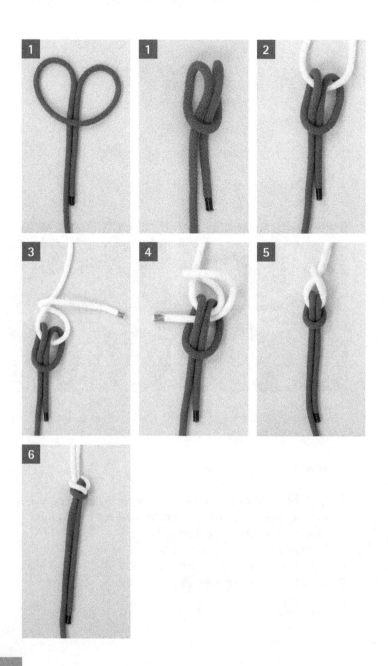

If you want to lengthen a double rope, that's just as simple:

1 Tie a secure knot in the end of one of the ropes.
2 Find the bight and wrap it around your fingers to create a running loop.
3 Now wrap this loop around the knot and pull it tight. Done!

Another alternative is to tie a cow hitch around an existing secure rope join.

The Science of Knots

I recently stumbled over an article in the German weekly *Die Zeit* on the science of knots. I was absolutely gobsmacked that there even was such a thing. In all seriousness, there are actual scientists researching whether you can unpick a knot even if after glueing the rope ends together. Me, I'm of a more practical bent. Learn some knots, pick up a hot dude, take him home, and wrap him up like a Christmas gift and then ... have fun!

▼ Single Limbs

This is Bernd's Super Knot. Our photo shows it tied around the model's arm, but you might want to practice tying it around your ankle. By placing your ankle on your knee you can keep both hands free for tying.

1 Find the bight, place around the limb, and pull the ends through.
2 Wrap the ends around the limb one more time and pull them through the loop.
3 Tighten.
4 Push one end through under the rope wrappings ...
5 Push the other end through the newly created loop ...
6 And pull tight.
7 Then just tie both ends together ...
8 And secure with a reef knot.

This knot will turn up regularly in our guide. It forms the basis of our ropework, so to speak, so practice it until you have it down pat, as you don't want to keep flipping back to this page.

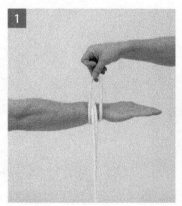
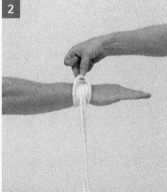

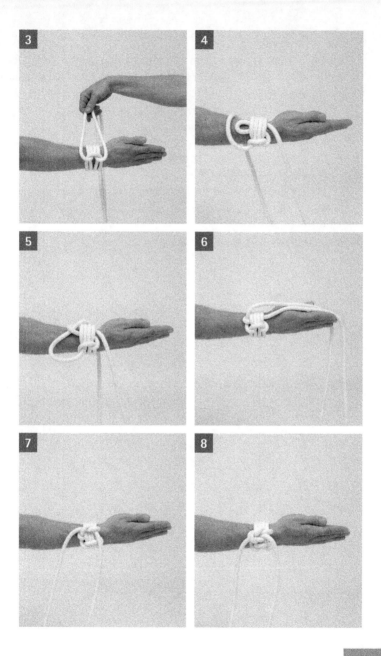

▼ Tying Limbs Together

Again, I'll show you how to do this with your ankles so that you can try this technique on yourself. First of all, ankles crossed. This is important for when you want to be able to reach and play with his cock.

If you take a look, you'll see that this is very similar to tying a single limb, with only one small addition.

1 Cross the ankles, draw the rope ends around the back and pull them through the loop in front.
2 Wrap the ends around the legs again (up to three or four times).
3 To prevent the ankles chafing, pull the ends *through* the legs several times ...
4 And secure with Bernd's knot.

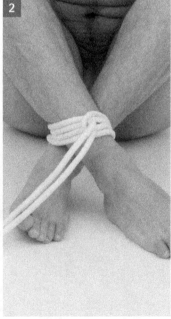

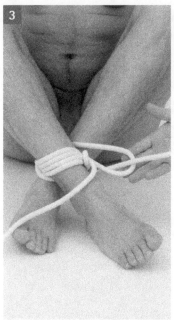

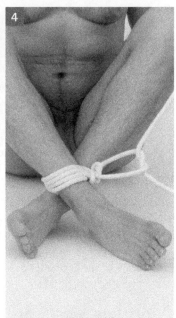

PS: If you tie the rope ends behind his neck, you can push him over on his side and play with him (provided you've already tied his arms!).

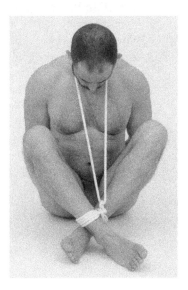

And now the legs again, but in a parallel tie. This is a useful technique if it's his behind you're after and you want the cheeks to stay spread.

1 Place the legs parallel to one another and wind a double rope around them at least twice, then pull the ends through the bight.
2 Now pass the right hand end back and under the ropes and pull it through the newly created loop in front.
3 Pull it tight, pass the rope back, under the ropes and through the loop again.
4 Repeat on the left hand side.
5 Once the feet are close enough together, secure both rope ends with a reef knot at the front.
6 Of course, it looks a lot better from this side. But you can take care of the aesthetics as soon as the technique is clear.

Uncoiling Long Ropes with One Hand

If you generally use the double rope technique, you should store your ropes like this: Bring the ends together and hold them, then wrap the double rope around your elbow and thumb. Finish by winding the bight around the coiled rope and pulling it through once.

To uncoil, hold onto the bight and throw the coil up and away from you. Then you can just go on knotting.

It is especially important to coil and store your ropes properly. If it gets tangled up when uncoiled, that tends to be a real downer during a bondage session.

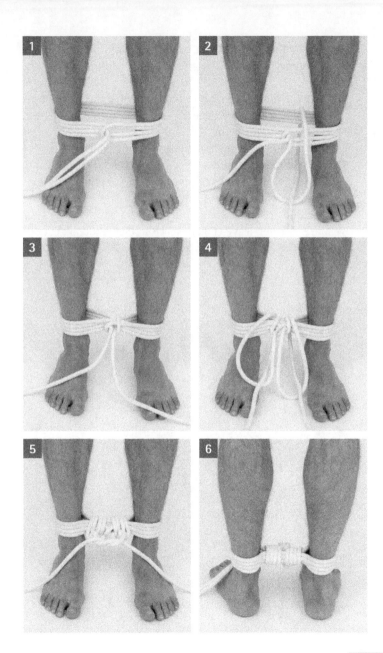

There is another way of tying someone's hands: in parallel. This is how it's done:

1 Place the forearms over one another behind the back and wind a double rope around them several times, then pull the free ends through the bight.
2 Now draw both ends through between the limbs ...
3 And pull them up on the other side. (If you tie the ends at the throat you've got yourself a nice restraint, but it's a bit uncomfortable because of the Adam's apple.)
4 Secure with Bernd's knot.
5 Make sure you leave enough space so that you don't cut off the circulation.

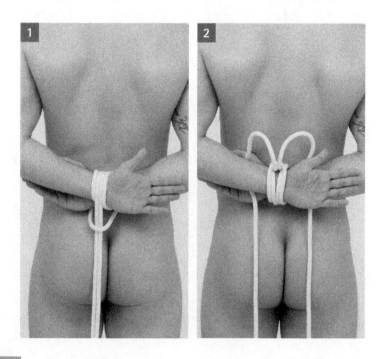

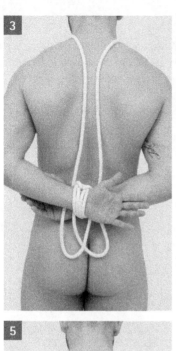

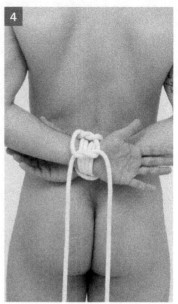

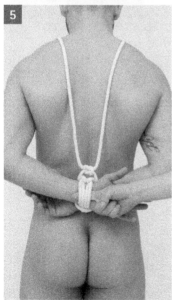

▼ Spread

A spread just means that the limbs are not tied close to each other but rather at a certain distance apart. You can, of course, use a bar to set the gap, but we don't want to neglect the purists here.

There's not much to explain. Just extend the limbs to slightly more than the desired distance, then wrap them several times using the double rope technique, pull the ends through the bight, and then tie the end on the right further and further away and do the same on the left. Done!

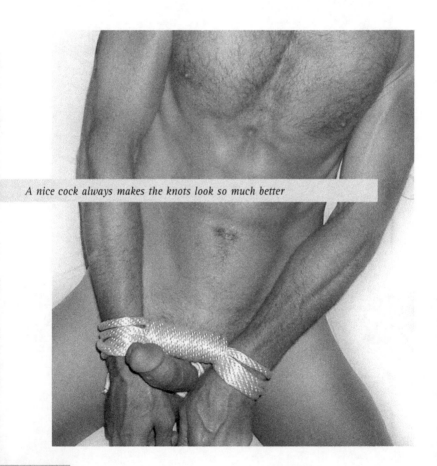

A nice cock always makes the knots look so much better

▼ Single Column Tie

This is useful if you want to tie your bottom's hands and feet to something. You can incoporate a loop, hang it on to something (for example, a St. Andrew's cross). Done.

1 Find the bight and wrap both ends of the doubled rope in parallel past each other around the wrist.
2 Place the bight over the rope wrappings.
3 Pull the front wrappings over the bight to the back.
4 Pull the bight through under the wrappings to the back ...
5 And then over the wrappings through the front loop.
6 Done!

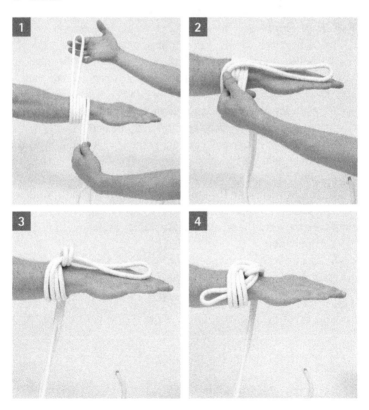

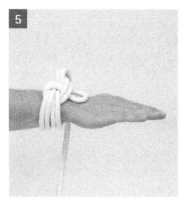 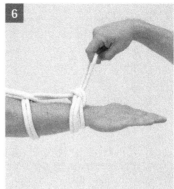

▼ Calf to Thigh

You'll need this for the fun sex positions listed from page 101 in this book, so pay close attention! Tying the calf to the thigh or the forearm to the upper arm is just as easy as tying a single limb.

1 Wrap the double rope around the calf and thigh three to four times and pull the rope ends through the bight.
2 Loosely push one end back under the knee, bring it back to the front under the transverse ropes, and pull it tight through the bight.
3 Do the same with the other rope end, only this time on the other side of the bight.
4 Repeat until the whole thing is secure, without cutting off the circulation.
5 Secure with a reef knot. Done.

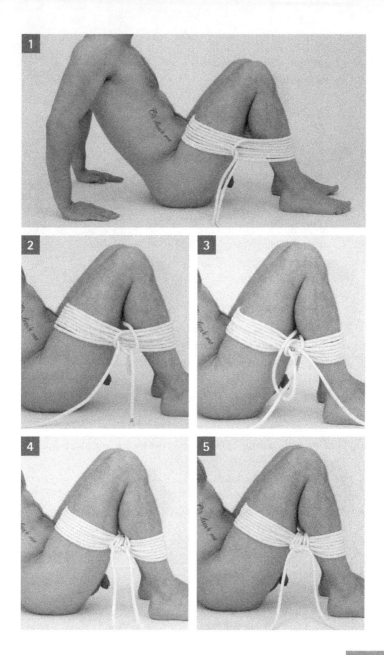

This photo of an arm binder should give you an idea (*illustration on the right*):

1 Find the bight and lay it on the outside in between the calf and the thigh on the outside, at the level of the ankles and the upper part of the thigh.

2 Then pass both rope ends in parallel around the calf and thigh and pull them through the bight.

3 Now pull both ends through the space between the calf and the thigh, wrap them round the rope on the inside of the thigh and pull them back through to the outside, while remaining parallel.

4 Draw them over the knots you've made and about 5 to 10 centimeters towards the knee ...

5 Then hold onto them with one hand and with the other, wrap them round the calf and thigh again, and then pull them through the part you're holding ...

6 Then back through the space between the calf and thigh,

7 Then back again (remaining parallel) ...

8 And through the knots, etc.

This tie, if performed securely and neatly, will withstand even long and intense tussling.

▼ What to Do with the End of the Rope?

Short ends can be tucked under to keep them out of the way. If you have longer ends, you can tie them into decorative shapes. This creates a pleasing effect and will also keep them from getting in your way. A professional rigger always knows where his ropework begins and where it ends. After all, he has to be able to untie it at a moment's notice.

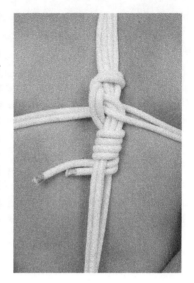

▼ Welts

Ropes will leave marks on a bound person's skin, there's no question about that. If that is a problem, bondage probably isn't for you. Here you can see the marks left by a simple body harness, worn for only about half an hour—and with no measures taken for added intensity. Generally, these are harmless. But if the welts turn blue, green, and red, or if they even start to bleed, you've probably overdone it.

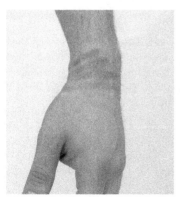
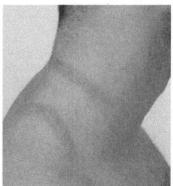

Self-Bondage

You can do bondage on your own as well. People tie themselves up, not (only) because they've no one to do it for them, but because it has its own special attractions.
As with partner play, there are different types of bondage. Some may enjoy the feeling of constriction, perhaps because it is similar to an embrace. Others may savor the pain it causes. Using genital bondag—which you can easily do to yourself—you can stretch your balls, tie off your dick to make it (even) harder, or delay orgasm.
With these forms of bondage you can always release yourself at any time.
But self-surrender also has its fans. They get a special kick out of putting themselves in a position of helplessness. And for this in particular they need to be on their own, without any kind of aid, even in an emergency.
The keys to handcuffs or padlocks holding the ropework together are placed somewhere where they can only be accessed with great difficulty, so that the practitioner can feel completely helpless—at least for a certain period of time.
Some practitioners create actual release mechanisms in order to prevent premature release. Timers are deployed, or elaborate constructions involving magnets and ropes are drawn through a candle so that you have to wait for the flame to sever them. Keys can be kept in a bucket of paint suspended from the ceiling, so that a release would precipitate the utter ruin of the room and its furnishings. Or you can freeze the key into a block of ice, so that it can't be reached until the ice has melted.
If you search the net, you will find scads of these stories. How many of them are actually true and how many merely the figments of their author's imagination, I am in no position to judge, having never experienced the slightest desire

for this sort of self-surrender. But one thing is clear: Over and over again, there will be people who have not been able to release themselves in time. Perhaps the mechanisms failed, or unexpected complications arose (a fit of coughing, nausea, a panic attack ...)

Self-bondage is perhaps one of the most dangerous sexual practices of all, especially if you add in breath control play (two words: autoerotic asphyxiation). Typical aids include plastic bags, damp fabric or gas and latex masks. While it is true that oxygen deprivation can increase sexual arousal during orgasm, a self-timer designed to prevent total asphixiation may well fail. Besides, as a bottom, you may get into trouble if you've tied yourself too tightly. Constricted limbs or fingers that have gone numb through insufficient circulation won't make untying knots any easier.

If my warning won't keep you from these practicing these life-endangering techniques, do me a favor and hide this book beforehand, so at least I won't have to read the tabloid headline "Niederwieser to blame!"

▼ Genital Bondage, Part 1

Now for the part most of our readers have probably been looking forward to from the very first page: a guide to attractive cock and ball ties, designed to give you a free hand with your favorite toy. (For reasons of hygiene, nylon, being both easy to clean and hard to tear, is the most suitable material for use in the genital area. You can also use leather ties.)

1   Lay the bight around your balls from the back and pull the ends through. But before you tie the knot ...
2   Pass the rope around a few more times, so that you have about 8 to 10 layers of rope. Then secure it with Bernd's knot. That's nice and tight and won't slip over your balls if you pull on it.
3   Now you can tie the ends to your toes, for example. That way, you'll have perfect control over the tension while you jerk off. Applied to the bottom, it means he won't be able to stand upright without a great deal of pain.
4   Use a knot you can untie quickly on your toes. This position is bound to cause thigh cramps.
5   You can intensify this by tying the rope to a calf. How long can he take it before falling over?
6   Use an easily untied knot for this, too: Pull the doubled rope around the leg and under the rope.
7   Then create a loop and pull it through the pre-existing loop. That way, the rope is secure enough so that it won't come undone by itself, but can be easily untied by pulling on it. (Of course, this type of knot won't hold for very long. Jiggling it a bit will make it come undone—not very well suited for your more recalcitrant slave.)

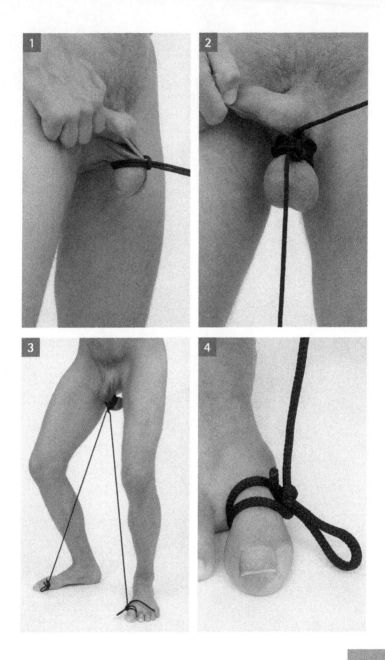

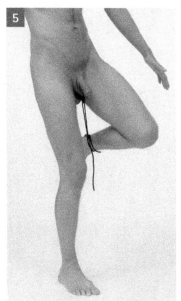

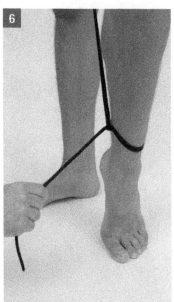

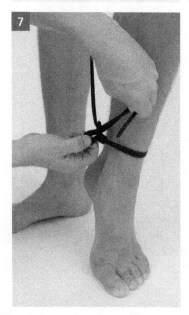

▼ Genital Bondage, Part 2

That was probably the simplest type of functional genital bondage I can think of. Now we can proceed further: not only stretching the balls, but wrapping them up.

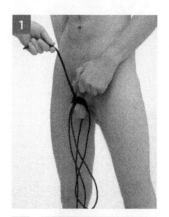

1 The same wrapping as before, only this time we pull the knot towards the back and pull the ends to the front, underneath the balls. Now thread them through the wrappings. (If you pull hard now, you'll give your bottom quite a rope burn. That will not only leave marks on his balls, it also hurts like hell.)

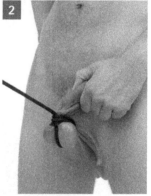

2 Now the balls are divided.
3 Here's a fun bit of torture: Tie knots in the rope and put them in your slave's mouth. He'd better not let go. It looks harmless enough, but try controlling your saliva flow for half an hour! Of course, you need to convince your slave beforehand that there'll be serious consequences should he drop the knot!

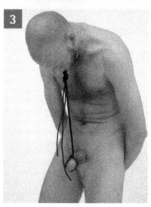

▼ Genital Bondage, Part 3

1. Start out with the original knot and then pull the ends upwards to the right and left, over your dick, cross them, and bring them back down.
2. Pull them under your dick ...
3. And cross them again over your dick. The result should look like this.
4. Now you can pull the ends up through your butt crack to your back ...
5. Over your pelvis and tie them on your abdomen.

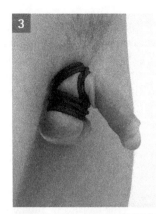

These examples are here to inspire you. Every cock and set of balls deserves its own individual decoration and treatment. You should first discuss whether your bottom is more interested in pain or in the aesthetic aspect. But as in this case you're playing and practicing by yourself, these questions should be easily resolved.

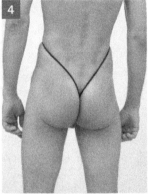

During all the fun and games, always make sure your junk (cock, balls) doesn't turn blue. While the genitals are very sensitive, oddly enough, we don't notice interrupted circulation. Before you know it, you've got yourself a bruise—rarely a pretty sight.

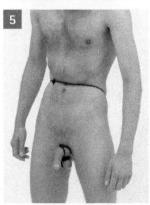

PS: And incidentally, don't panic if Mr. Happy loses interest during the proceedings. This is due less to your (as yet) incompetence, and more to the fact that your mind is currently occupied with getting the knots right. As soon as you have mastered these, you'll be rewarded with an incredible pleasure gain. So, keep going. No slacking!

▼ Chastity Bondage, Part 1

Chastity does not only play a role in S-M. Many non-S-M practitioners enjoy having the ability to get an erection taken from them. It's a mind fuck in every sense of the word. You are being aroused by the inability to get aroused. It's unreal when you think about it. And that's why it's hot.

The simplest version is ...

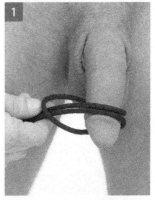

1 Lay a loop around the glans and pull the ends through, so that the loop lies on the frenulum.
2 Pull it tight. Done.

Once again, the whole thing is attached to the feet. Or to the floor, if you've tied your partner to a St. Andrew's cross, etc. You can be really nasty and pull your dick back into your butt crack. Not only does that prevent an erection, it also looks pretty unattractive (a bit like a swollen pussy).

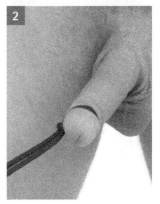

PS: This act is also very useful if you want to interrupt an orgasm. Just press hard below the glans, and the party's over.

▼ Chastity Bondage, Part 2

For something more elaborate ...

1 Lay the loop along the length of the erect penis (with the bight up front on the glans).
2 Then pull the rope at the back of the shaft around under your dick and wrap it around the entire length up to the front ...

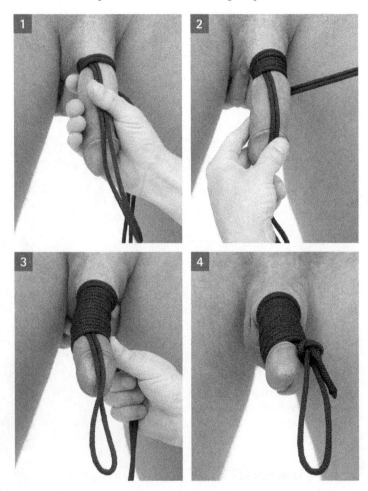

3 Until your boner is completely covered. Make sure the ropes lie flat next to each other.

4 When you reach the front part, tie a knot. And that will give you a fixed loop which you can attach to another rope or whatever takes your fancy. A dog leash is another possibility, but I don't want to give you ideas.

Always remember to massage the affected parts after genital bondage to restore circulation. After all, we don't want them damaged ...

▼ **Pelvis**

The straight man's garter belt is presumably the gay man's crotch rope.

If a trussed-up pelvis spells ecstasy to you, just follow these simple instructions:

1 Lay a simple loop around the cock and balls.

2 Pull the ends back over the pelvis towards the back and tie a reef knot. This will prevent the loop from tightening. (If your muffin top prevents you from being able to find your pelvic bones, crotch ropes aren't for you.)

3 Pull the rope through your butt crack to the front.

4 Pull it back again over the loins.

5 Thread it through the lower ropes and pull it back to the front ...

6 And around the thighs to the back ...

7 Where you knot the ends.

8 And isn't that nice?

Of course, we're just getting started. A professional will know all sorts of things you can do with this simple construction, but I really ought to leave some things to your imagination.

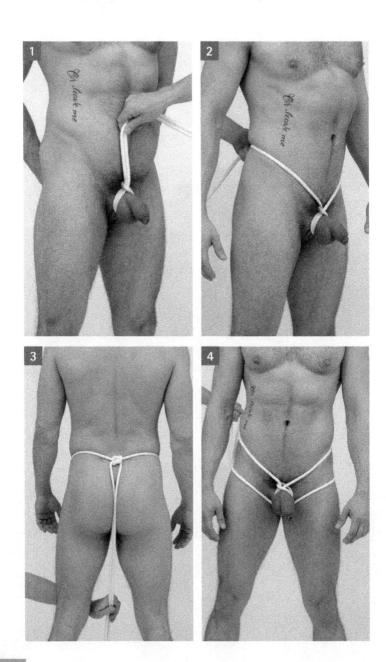

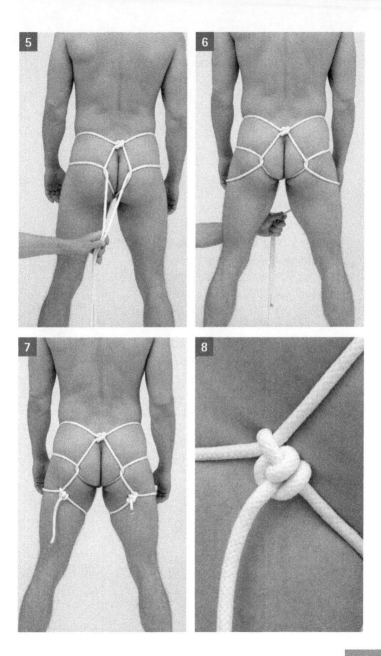

▼ Tying Limbs to Objects

As a final preparatory measure, I'll show you how to attach a bar to your body. This has many benefits. The *pau de arara* is presumably well known as a torture device (if not, just read the Wikipedia article—actually, don't). It is also often used in S-M. But a bar can also be of use in other types of bondage not particularly geared towards pain.

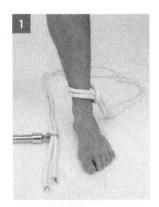

If you're using a bar with attached cuffs (available from most sex toy shops or homemade with hardware store materials), it's relatively simple: you just thread the ropes through the cuffs. If you prefer to work with wood or bamboo, you can attach the rope to the bar with a lark's head (see above), before proceeding with the ropework.

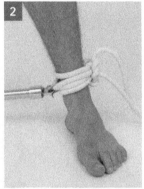

1   Place the bight around a leg (as before), then pull the free rope ends through the cuffs or the D-rings.
2   And then proceed with your tie, again as before. Make sure the metal doesn't press too hard against the skin and especially the bones, as not even the staunchest slave will be able to stand it for long.

3 Now tie the other foot to the bar the same way and the legs will be nicely spread.

Now you're all set. Anything else is just a combination of the ties you've just read about. Actually, I could already let you set out into the exciting world of ropes from here, but don't worry: I'll accompany you for a bit longer. In the next chapter I'll be showing you the ten most exciting bondage positions for sex.

▼ Gags

We'll conclude with some instructions for a small gag. Gags fulfill all sorts of purposes. In pain play, this is self-evident, but a gag will also increase a slave's feeling of helplessness. His mouth will fill with saliva and his cries will be stifled ...

Gags are some of the most popular sex toys, which is why you can buy them in all shapes and sizes, but as a purist you may want to work solely with ropes. In that case, I've got just the thing for you:

1 Use a 3 meter rope to make a loop as illustrated and adjust according to mouth size.
2 Pull the top end under the lower rope, like a hangman's noose.
3 Now wrap the rope around tightly, over and over again, until you reach the end of the loop.
4 Once there's only a tiny loop left, thread the end through.
5 Now pull the other (!) end of the rope tight. Done!
6 Secure behind the head with a reef knot. Of course, this sort of gag can also be incorporated into facial bondage, to great effect.

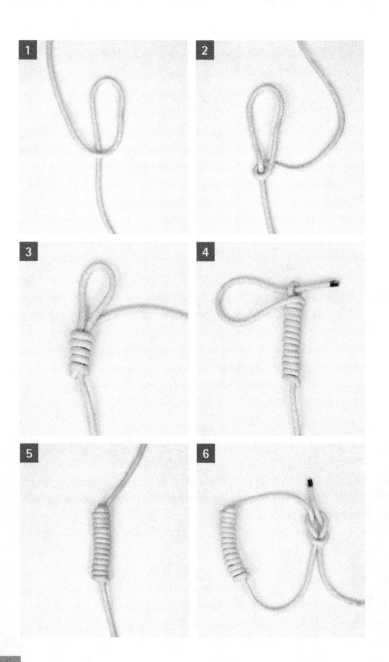

PS: If you're using a cotton rope (which I can only advise, as it is much more pleasant to bite down on), you can refine it by adding all kinds of flavors: peppermint, coffee, urine ...

An Overview of the Key Points

If you are leafing through this book and deciding whether or not to buy it according to what's in the boxes, then go for it! You won't learn much just by reading. Practice, practice, practice! If you want to start off small, start off with the reef knot and Bernd's knot. These are the most important ones. Once you have mastered them, the rest is a piece of cake.

But I really want to strongly emphasize: Bondage is a dangerous practice. Understanding the effects of complex ties beforehand isn't easy. You will need loads of practice and finesse. So, I can't emphasize this enough: practice on yourself! That way, you can practice the knots and at the same time perceive their effect on your senses, your skin, and on your mind—and your understanding of this exciting and rewarding technique will increase.

Once you have immobilized your partner with the aid of ropes ...

The Best Positions (for Sex)

Bondage is art. It's meditation, communication—and of course, it's a great form of sexual foreplay, interlude, or even the main act. In this chapter I will show you how a few ropes can help you have (even more) thrilling sex.

Being able to tie knots is all well and good. But it's even better if you combine your rope play with a game of hide-the-bologna. Which is why I've selected ten positions that are wonderfully suited to fucking and sucking, without being too complicated. These are just an introduction, a kind of sample. Once you have mastered them, you will have no problem setting up more elaborate bondage routines.

While in the last chapter on knot work I made sure to include exercises you can try out and practice on yourself, for this chapter you will need a playmate. You can safely promise him that he will be duely rewarded for his efforts.

▼ Foreplay

Yes, you shouldn't leave out foreplay in bondage either. Having witnessed a number of sessions, I was always very impressed when the players managed to establish real contact. Of course, that is a matter of taste. Some may find being tied up in a cool and unemotional manner more arousing.

Look into his eyes. Give your partner the feeling that you are really aware of him. Scan his body from head to toe. This kind of non-verbal communication will help you establish a feeling for each other, forming the basis for any sort of trust.

Now touch him, embrace him, hold him tight from behind or lay him down in your lap. You can carefully shift his weight to see how far he will let himself go, how far he trusts you, leans on you, will let himself be led by you.

Take your time. And of course, kissing, nipple stroking, licking his neck, and letting him feel your hot breath will also fire up your sexual arousal for both of you.

Incorporate the ropes into getting to know one another. Draw them over his body, shake them close to his ear and let him hear them, draw them beneath his nose and let him smell them (carefully, you don't want to injure the delicate skin above his upper lip). And depending on what you're both aiming for (this time I mean how rough you both want this to get), you can up the ante: grab him more roughly, push him, shove him, etc.

Alternately, if hard S-M is what you're both up for, you can leave out the physical contact altogether. It is enough to stand facing each other, the slave held captive in the master's gaze. If he still unperturbedly measures the rope with his hands, then show him who's boss.

The Setting

Of course, all the trappings also depend on what you're playing. You might not need that scented oil burner for S-M play, nor is a dark BDSM club necessarily the best place for a sensual tantric session.

It pays to think about the following: temperature (if you're naked and relaxed, you'll get cold easily—might be just the thing for your slave?), music, candles (preferably ones suitable for wax play), scents (and I don't just mean poppers), flooring (soft, hard, warm, comfortable ...), keep ropes and toys at hand, don't forget the condoms and lube. Glucose tablets and drinks. Turn off the ringer on your cell phone but keep it on hand in case of emergencies.

Getting to know the other person: kissing, stroking, and observing his reactions

▼ Chest Harness

This simple chest harness also forms an essential part of larger-scale bondages, for example, suspensions.

1　Pass the double rope around the back of his neck, with the bight dangling at around belly button level.
2　Turn him around and pull the ends under his arms and through the bight.
3　Pull the ends back to the front ...
4　Then back again and thread them through the bight.
5　This is the front view so far. But we're not done yet.
6　Now wrap the rope around his rib cage in the opposite direction to the back.

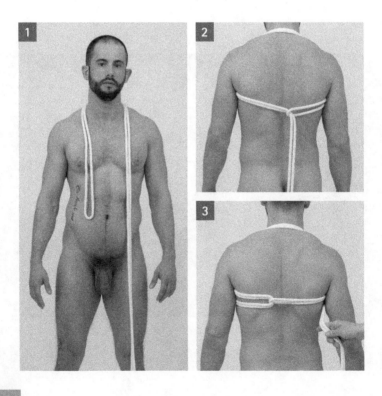

7 Pull the bight up from the other side.
8 Pull it through the neck rope.
9 Let it drop down and then pull it through the bight again.

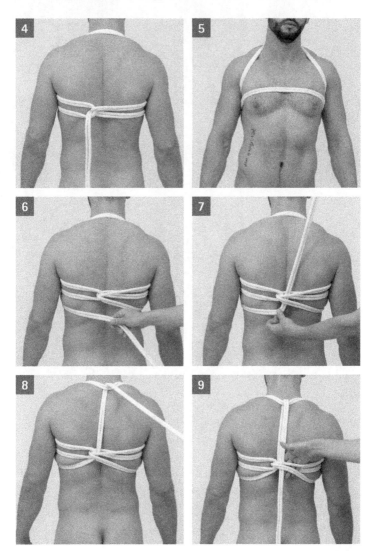

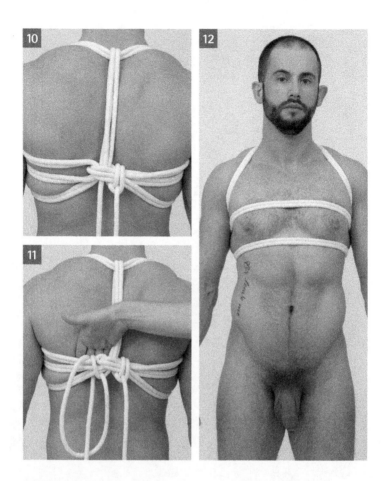

10 Secure everything with a hitch ...
11 On the left and on the right hand side.
12 The hands, etc., can now be tied to this harness.

PS: Accentuate the nipples by tying the ropes tightly around them. You can also tie off the nipples and simply attach the rope ends to the harness.

▼ Combinations

The chest harness can, of course, be beautifully complemented by a crotch rope (see the guide to knots). The two ties can then be connected in all sorts of ways. You can tie in the wrists or the legs, in which case a reef knot will stand you in good stead.

The "spread-eagle" section on page 113 will show you how to tie someone's wrists or ankles. And by all means, the genitals can be beautifully incorporated into this game. So can chastity bondage ...

▼ Facial Bondage

Before we get to the positions you can create by combining what you've learned so far, just a short excursion into the world of binding the senses, for as you are (hopefully) aware, taking away or even just inhibiting one sense can dramatically change one's physical sensations. Not being able to see what your partner is doing, feeling only the fluttering air caused by his movements, can be quite exciting.

In my experience, it can be even more exciting to have a gag stifling the cries in your throat, to be able to really yell as you normally wouldn't be able to do in a rented apartment without at best alerting the neighbors, if not the police. And believe you me, yelling is incredibly hot.

If you want to stick to the easy stuff, you can just use a hood or a face mask. There is an enormous selection of these available from any good toy store (see chapter *Tools and Aids*, page 166). But in this chapter we will be concerning ourselves with the possible uses of ropes:

You can use an exercise band secured with a rope to wrap the eyes and ears (you do know not to put too much pressure on the eyes, right?). Silk ties can also be used. Or leather. And now for a special type of facial bondage. The result is a sort of head-cage, only with ropes instead of rigid bars.

Facial bondage is always a bit scary for a beginner to handle. But as it looks great and is something rather special, even for a professional, I've decided to include it in this manual so that you can really impress people. Perhaps not at your next book club meeting, but definitely at the next fetish party in Berlin ...

Before you start wrapping your partner up, you need to take a few

Close mesh netting or well-placed ropes will make the bottom feel especially well supported.

measurements of his head. Ropes over the eyes look like s**t. Nor should they be placed over the ears, as this can also be very painful. Ropes will sit nicely over the chin, the upper lip, and the eyebrows.

In this case, a 6 mm rope, 3 meters long will suffice.

1   Hook the middle of the rope under his chin and pull it back over the head. Then tie a double coin knot at eyebrow level. It should sit underneath the base of the skull, otherwise it will hurt and it won't look good.
2   Now tie a double coin knot at the back in the soft hollow under the base of the skull.
3   Pull the ends under the ears towards the front and through the loop under the chin. Pull them apart to the left and the right.
4   Next step: Now pull the ropes back again, parallel to the lines you just made going forward. Thread them through the knots at the back.
5   Now pull them forwards over his ears to the double coin knot between his eyebrows ...
6   And thread them through.
7   Pull the ropes upwards over the forehead and secure them on top of his head like this: First pull one end through under the two ropes that are already on top of his head ...
8   Then repeat from the other side with the other end.
9   Secure with a reef knot.
10 And now you have a net from which you can safely suspend a head.

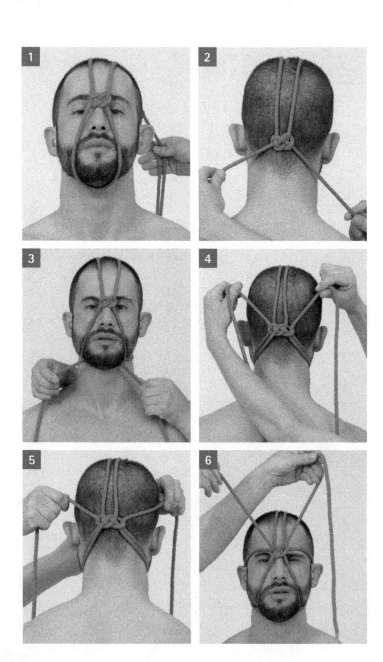

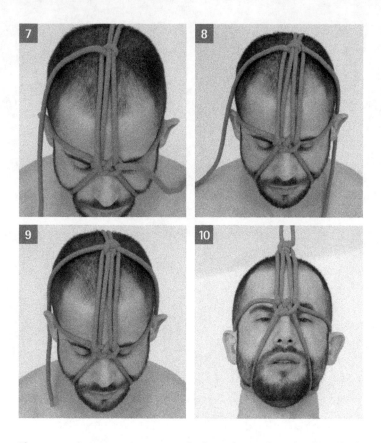

If you attach your partner not only from the top but also from both sides, so that he no longer needs to hold up his head himself, this can be very relaxing. But you can also do this with a view to making him even more helpless ...

▼ Earplugs

As simple as they are, never underestimate the effect earplugs can have. As the mind will already be geared towards a heightened consciousness under strain, inhibiting the senses will radically change his perception.

A spread-eagle on his back: the family jewels are easily accessible

The Best Bondage Positions for Sex

Right, now you're all set for the big finale: positions involving the entire body. Here is a selection of those well suited for sex.

▼ Spread-eagle

This is a great position, if only because it's so versatile. It can be done lying down, standing up, hanging if necessary, on your front and on your back. Additionally it has the great advantage of being virtually impossible to escape from—unless you have snake fingers. Not least, a man in a spread position like this is an ideal plaything, as his entire body is defenseless—see our illustration. And now, step by step:

1 Tie the bottom's ankles and wrists with a single column tie.
2 A quick reminder: Wrap the doubled rope around the wrist two, or preferably three, times and pull the ends through the bight.

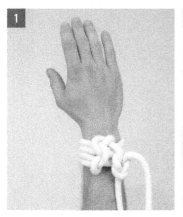
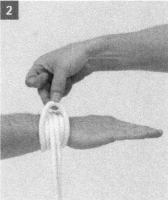

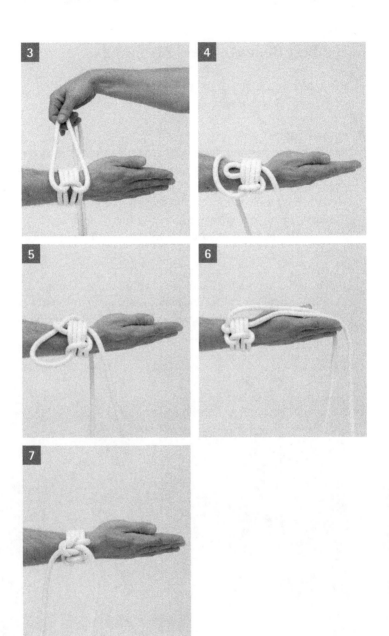

3 Divide the ends.
4 Push one end under the wrappings, forming a loop on the other side.
5 Thread the other end through this loop.
6 Pull both ends tight ...
7 And secure with a reef knot.

Now you'll need something secure to tie the rope ends to. Bedposts are generally readily available. The legs of bed will work too, if necessary, although you can't tie the limbs down too tightly because of the mattress, giving the bottom more room to maneuver.

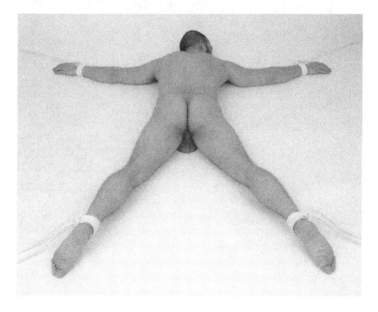

Another alternative is the St. Andrew's cross—if you have one. As a rule, this is the better option if it is large enough, as the bottom won't be able to reach the knots to release himself. A sturdy wardrobe is a great alternative to the St. Andrew's cross, especially one with mirrored doors.

Hooks on the walls and ceiling are a conceivable option—large rooms would require longer ropes. An attractive possibility would be to spread your slave out between four table legs under a table— and then, of course, to invite guests over for dinner. They could always sit down to dinner in the nude and possibly relieve themselves on him ...

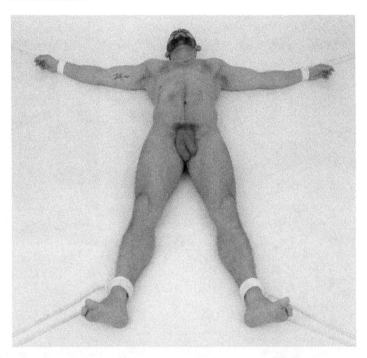

Ah, memories ...

PS: Remember, you can use the spread-eagle position to restrain your sub either bottom- or belly-up, so that your favorite side is free for you to play with. If you have large double wing doors, of course, that leaves both the front and back free ...

Doing it standing up: a spread-eagle on a St. Andrew's cross

Warmup Exercises

In order to be able withstand longer periods of strain or keeping still without sustaining injury, it can be helpful to keep the muscles flexible with yoga or exercise. This advice is aimed in particular at those men who go to the gym to toughen their muscles up, which as a rule results in a loss of flexibility.

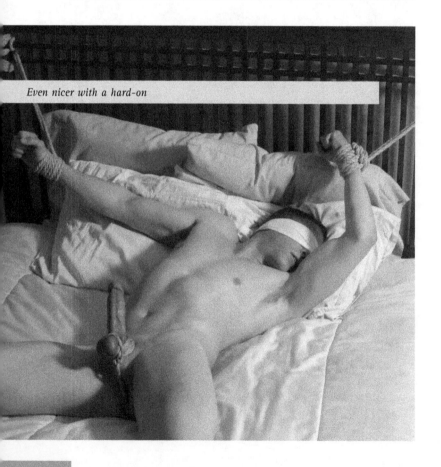

Even nicer with a hard-on

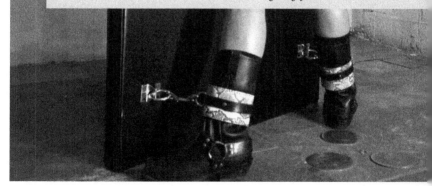

If you don't have a St. Andrew's cross, just attach a hook to the wall, giving you access to his ass.

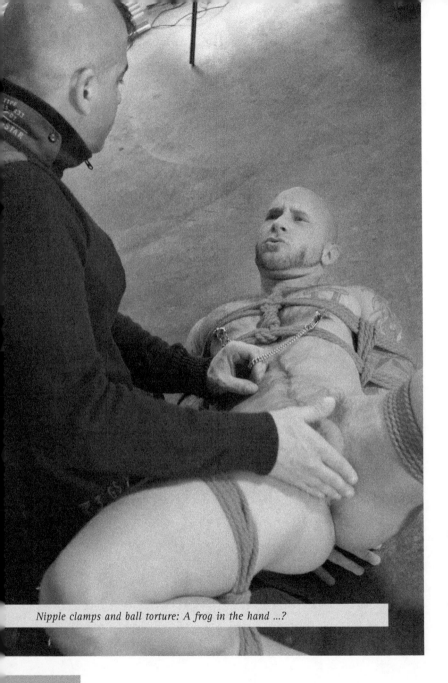

Nipple clamps and ball torture: A frog in the hand ...?

▼ Frogtie

You might call this position "A frog he would a-wooing go!", or more to the point, "a-fucking"!

If you want to take him by surprise, have him sit on the floor. That way, he'll have no idea what he's in for.

1   This time, spread the feet further apart (you'll want enough space between them later on). They can be further apart than pictured here.

2   Then restrain his arms behind his head by tying his upper and lower arms together. You could tie them behind his back, but later on—as soon as he lies on his back—he won't be able to keep that up for long. And you might want to spend just a little more time with him ...

3   You can secure his arms behind his neck with a rope pulled through both arm bindings ...

4   If you want to make absolutely sure he can't escape, use the hand-on-top-of-each-other technique from our chapter on knots.

5   Then tie his thighs to his calves, leaving you with a deliciously wrapped package.

6   Finish by tipping him over on his back—and your froggy is ready for action.

7   You can go one better by tying his arms above his head, for example, to the headboard of the bed. You can attach his legs to the wall with ropes off at both sides, creating an ideal position (for you). That way, you can regulate the height of his legs. (I don't know what you're planning to do with him ...)

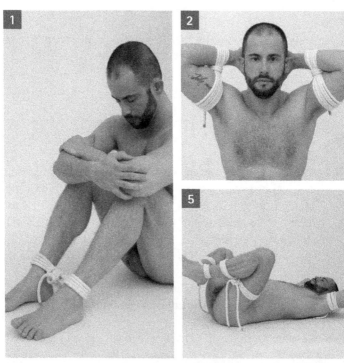

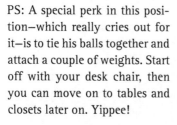

PS: A special perk in this position—which really cries out for it—is to tie his balls together and attach a couple of weights. Start off with your desk chair, then you can move on to tables and closets later on. Yippee!

Use the hogtie to force him to his knees: What for?
You'll think of something.

▼ Hogtie

The name is originally taken from American farmers, who would capture and tie up their animals (hogs, but the same thing works on calves, too) with their lassoes so that they could stamp a brand mark into the soft ass-flesh. But I'm not trying to give you ideas ...

1 Start off with a chest harness while standing up (see page 104).
2 Then tie his legs together at the ankles.
3 Have him lie down on his stomach like that.
4 Don't forget his hands: After all, the general idea here is to completely immobilize him.

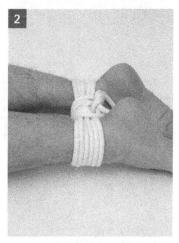

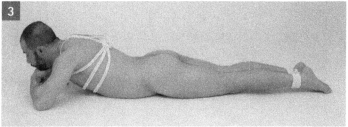

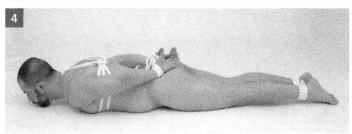

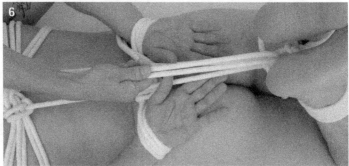

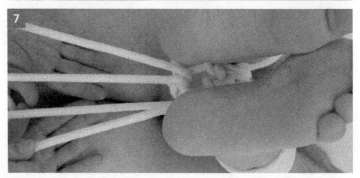

5 Now attach a long rope to the chest harness using a cow hitch.
6 Pull the ends through the wrist cuffs ...
7 And through the ankle cuffs.

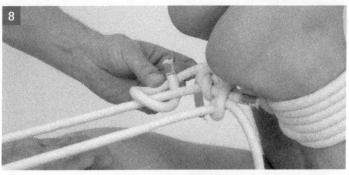

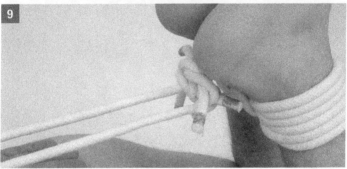

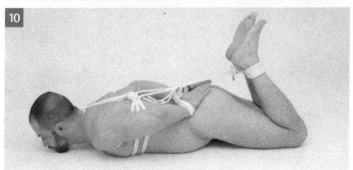

8   Pull the rope back over the top and then through the loop from underneath.
9   Secure with a reef knot.
10 And there's your neatly wrapped package.

Sauve qui peut! A poorly tied up bottom can always protect himself.

Obviously you can't do much to your partner sexually in this position, but try pushing him over so that he's lying on his side, and now he just has to suck any dick that gets pushed down his throat. His own dick is equally defenseless.

In S-M you might add some punching into the mix, or kick your slave in the stomach with your boots. This isn't really my thing. As a health practitioner, I can't help but think of the possible health risks: organs tearing, bruising, etc.

PS: This is the beginner's version. Once you've had some practice, you'll be able to do this a lot faster and simpler. A professional does not need to rely on the bottom's cooperation. They just throw a lasso over him, sit on his chest, and tie up all fours, like a lamb to the slaughter, then load up and ... well, use your imagination.

Run a Tight Ship

As I've said before, you and your partner should agree on the type of bondage play beforehand. But one thing is certain, if you don't pull the ropes nice and tight, if they just lie slackly around your bottom's limbs and he can move just as well as if they weren't there at all, then ... well, I don't know either.

Completely defenseless. But water is just for starters.

▼ Chair Bondage

Take a short break ... every office should be equipped with at least one chair. Chair bondage is suitable especially if a bottom tries to switch to top, in the sense of tying the top up, sucking him off hard and then sitting on his dick. That way, the bottom determines how he wants to be fucked. A badly behaved bottom won't let the top cum, instead he'll wait until the last minute and then leave his dick standing (literally). Preferably right before the next board meeting. You'd never hear the end of it. (By implication, this also means: Never let anyone tie you up at the office unless you're completely sure they're well-disposed towards you ...)

A really bitchy bottom will sit on the top with his back turned, so that the top can't watch as he plays with his dick while he uses the top as a dildo up his ass, and then shoots his load all over the desk instead of decorating his nipples with it. Not cool.

In contrast to the illustration on the left, we used a mid-century classic for our (photo) shoot, just to show you that you don't have to rely on a particular type of chair. To the attentive viewer it might bring to mind the James Bond movie in which the delectable Daniel Craig is tethered to a chair and subjected to ball torture. Very porny! (This is not meant as an invitation!)

1   Tie the ankle to the chair leg with a short rope (2 meters). Make sure to leave a gap, otherwise it will quickly become painful. The horizontal join will restrain and immobilize the foot.
2   If you're using longer ropes, you can use the rest to tie his arms to the arms of the chair.
3   Next, do the same with the thighs, so that he can't close his legs. After all, you want to be able to reach his cock, right?
4   A chest tie can't hurt, otherwise he might lean forwards and bite you. Unless that's your thing.
5   At this point, malicious minds might come up with a noose around his neck which could be joined to human or chair legs under the chair. But—I'll gladly repeat myself here—forget the neck nooses! These little things have injured many a good man.

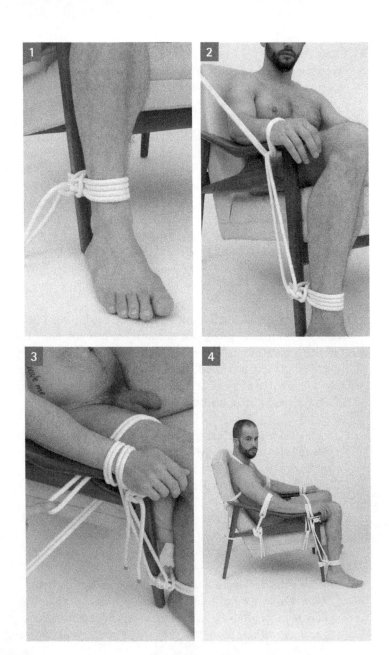

PS: A recalcitrant bottom should be tied to the arms of the chair by the hands, so he doesn't get in your way when you're doing the other ties.

Of course, this is just one way of combining a man and a chair to an erotic whole, among many, many others. The final work of art will depend on the chair and its individual shape, which will also determine the attachment points. It will also depend on what your partner's body can stand, or to put it more kindly, what it appreciates ...

Teardrop: another kind of sex swing

▼ Teardrop

The name is derived from the resulting shape: your man is suspended from the ceiling by a rope; above him only the thin rope—and his body below. But the name could also be a metaphor: You will be moved to tears at the sight of a naked man hanging from the ceiling ...

1 Tie the legs together with enough space in between, so that the ankles aren't pressed together when he is suspended.
2 Now tie the arms together at the same distance.

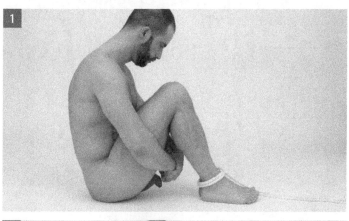

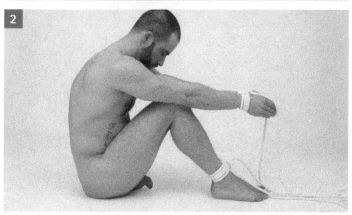

3   Now pull both rope ends from the arm ties through the ankle ties.
4   Now the other way around, pull the rope ends from the ankle
     ties through the arm ties. Pull the whole thing tight to make it
     nice and secure.
5   To finish: Lay the bottom on his back under the ceiling hook
     and hang him up by all four ropes.
6   And now it's time to shed a tear.

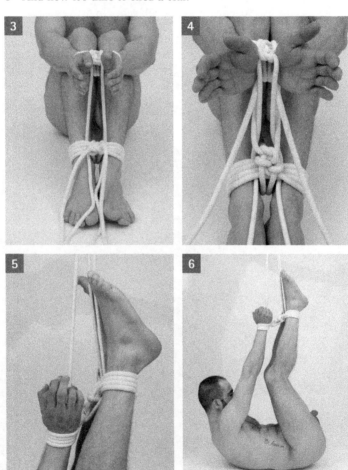

PS: Do you see how wonderfully defenseless his genitals are in this position?

I know you're moved, but don't let that stop you from keeping a constant eye on the bottom. You're a beginner. If your ankle ties aren't absolutely perfect, they might tighten and cut off his circulation, which will be painful. If his hands and feet turn blue, you'll know he's long overdue for release.

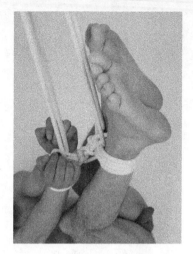

Incidentally, this position is only for quickies, not being the most comfortable for longer periods of time. Aside from the hand and foot ties, all but the most athletic backs will soon begin to ache and most people will appreciate how very difficult it is to hold your head up like that for long.

Having read this book attentively, you will no doubt immediately come up with a way to make this more comfortable for the bottom. That's right: using a head harness (facial bondage), hung stably, to take the load off the neck.

Neck Bondage
All positions that put strain on the neck are extreme positions. The bottom won't be able to sustain these for more than a few minutes without their resulting in pain, tension, or eventually a trapped nerve. Here in our studio, we had expert supervision from someone with years of experience, someone who basically does nothing but wrap people up in ropes. So, he knows what he's doing.

The Y-position, pictured here with lateral traction cuffs in place of the spreader bar

▼ The Y-Position

If you don't have a St. Andrew's cross but would still like to fondle the lower parts of your helpless playmate, here's a fine, very simple and effective alternative.

1   Lay the bight around one ankle as before.
2   Then, before you wrap the double rope around the leg the second time, first pull it through the bar. If the bar presses painfully against the joint (and your bottom doesn't enjoy that), you can also attach the bar to the rope afterwards, for example, using a carabiner connector. (You can take care of him standing up or sitting down. Not everyone can stand easily with their legs apart, as this makes it difficult to adjust your balance).

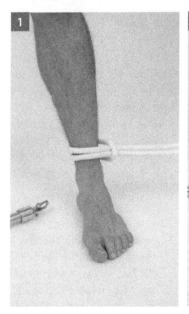
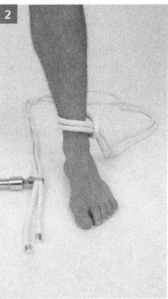

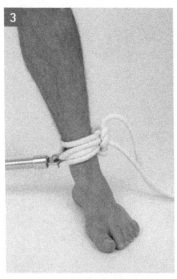

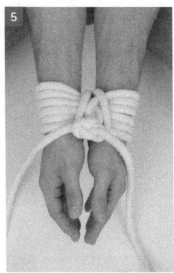

3 Tie it up ... done!

4 Just repeat with the other ankle—now his legs are spread so far he won't able to fend off your attacks. But ... his hands are still free. We'll have to do something about that.

5 Have your bottom stretch out his arms forward and tie them with Bernd's knot.

6 If he is sitting down, carefully help him up, then pull the arm ropes through the ceiling hook and secure them. Now he's ready to play.

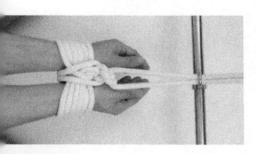

You can also pull the arm rope through the cuff in the middle of the bar, secure it and then have your guy stand on all fours. See him raise his ass to the skies ... beautiful!

6

A pleasurable pau de arara: *like so many other bondage techniques, originally a form of torture*

▼ Dogtie

Everyone is familiar with the wonderful doggie position, so here's a bondage version. Just tie the legs together at the ankles and tie the wrists, then tip your guy over forwards and bingo! His ass, in all its magnificence, is at your disposal. Hopefully you'll know what to do with it without further explanation, but if not: read up on it in *Bend Over! The Complete Guide to Anal Sex.* But first things first:

1 Have him sit on the floor naked.
2 Tie his feet first. Preferably spread (can be further apart than pictured here), so that you can kneel between his legs later on. (You should already be familiar with this tie, otherwise please read page 121).
3 Then have him place his arms on his knees with his arms at the same distance as his feet. Tie him up in this spread.
4 Now push him over onto all fours.
5 Tie the upper arms to the thighs. Again, you can use the usual tie (don't tie into the joints as there are very sensitive nerves there. You risk causing numbness, a premature end to your session and possible long-term damage.)
6 Isn't that a lovely sight?

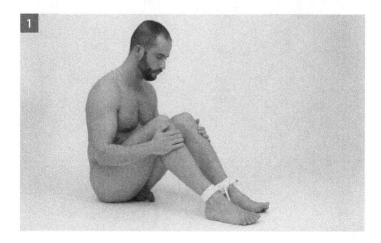

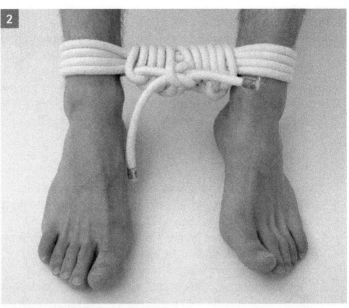

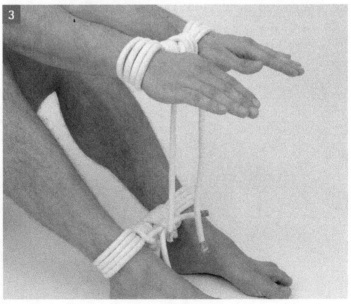

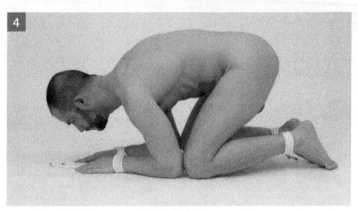

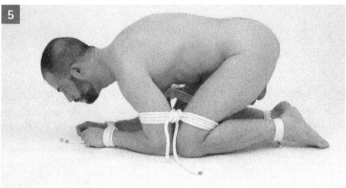

If you're tying him to the bed, you can secure the leg and arm ties to the bedpost or the frame, so that he's completely restrained and fully immobilized. Additionally, he will be unable to reach the knots to release himself.

PS: Another variation is to turn him on his back and attach him to the ceiling with ropes at the front and back. Another great rear entry.

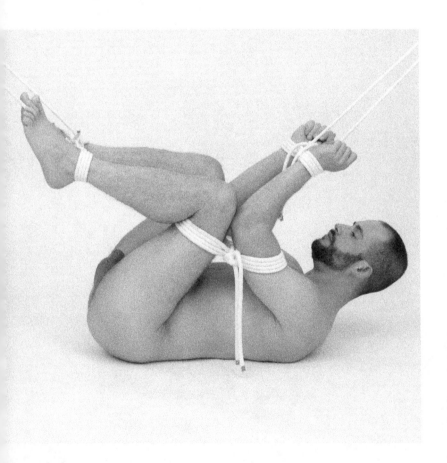

For More Stimulation

Of course, there is no law that says you can't play with your tethered bunny in a variety of ways. Vibrators are an option. Want to be really cruel? Get your little bundle all turned on till he's ready to explode and then take the vibrator away from him at the last moment.

For those unaware of nipple play, let me remind you that stimulating these little pink buds will cause a release of oxytocin, which not only makes you happy and content, but is also known as the bonding (sic!) hormone. This medical term does not however refer to bondage, but to human bonding, originally the maternal bond between a mother and her newborn child.

If your relationship with your mother was a difficult one, you might prefer to use nipple clamps. No, I'm just kidding. But some people may eschew fondling and a sense of well being in favor of pain, the more excruciating, the better. Nipple clamps are just the beginning. Whipping might be a successful follow-up.

And have you ever dripped hot wax over someone's tender skin?

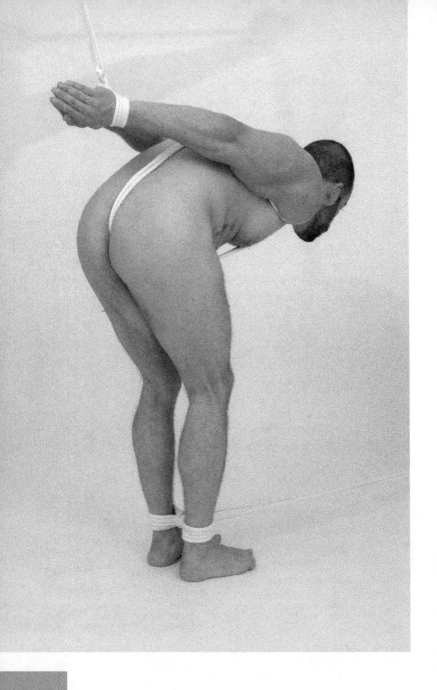

▼ Curtsey

This time, it's all in the name (not in the metaphor). This position again exposes the rear end, but its actual aim is to humiliate the bottom by forcing him to endure a "girly" pose. You can exacerbate this by exposing him to the derision of others, for example, at a Christmas party. That way, you can teach the little ones how to wrap their presents nicely. No, there's no way I can let this joke stand. I'll delete it. I promise!

1 Have your bit of man candy stand up and begin by tying his legs together. Don't forget to leave a small gap so as not to hurt his ankles!

2 Tie his arms together at the wrists behind his back. It's best to use a long rope for this, because ...

3 Then you pull the rope, and with it the arms up to the ceiling hook and force the bottom to his knees.

4 For the curtsey: Pull the loop from his back under one arm, over the back of the neck and under the other arm, then pull the ends through the loop and pull them tight.

5 Draw the ends through the loop at the back of the neck and pull them downwards.

6 Draw them through the loop again and then pull them back through the crotch.

7 Pull them up behind the the back of the neck, drawing the head down.

8 Pull them back through the crotch ...

9 And attach them to the knot at the back, so that the neck is bent at the desired angle.

10 Secure with a knot.

11 If there's any rope left, wrap it round neatly. We want to make a good impression.

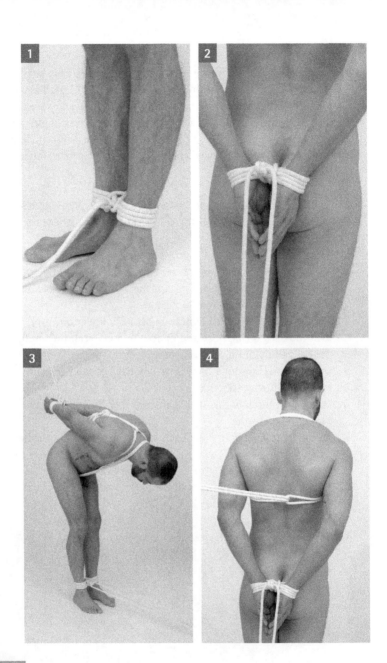

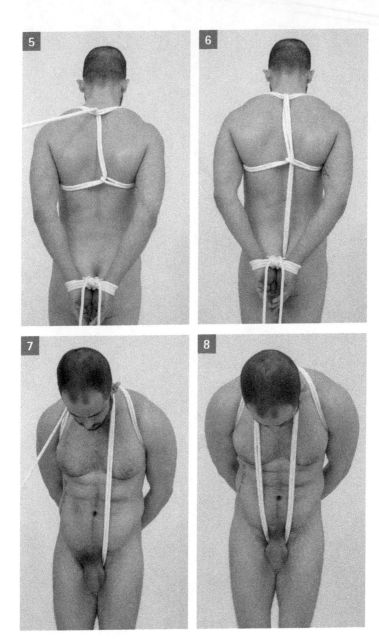

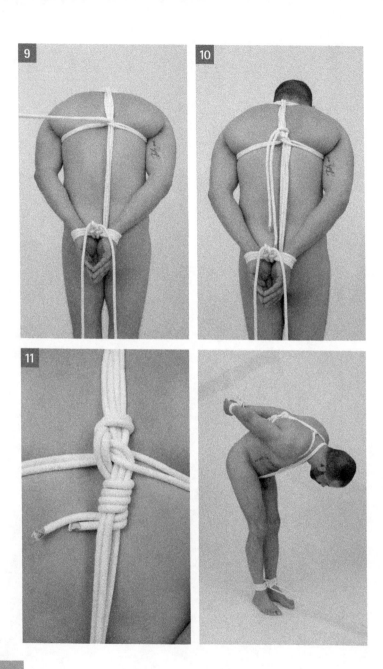

Alternatively, to ensure his head is humbly bowed, you can simply tie the head into the curtsey. To do this, place the bight around the back of his neck and pull the ends back through the legs and up to the ceiling hook. The stronger the pull, the deeper the curtsey. But a single rope will make this a lot more uncomfortable and result in a stiff neck!

Now you can invite a few guests over to enjoy the spectacle. Surprise!

PS: Bondages involving the neck are not suitable for beginners, but are rather a goal to aim for.

Bound—and Now What?

Well, what happens once you've tied someone up and suspended him from the ceiling? Do you suck him, fuck him, or fist him? That's just one option. As a beginner you might just be content to have got it done right. For me, the real pleasure in bondage lies in continuously improving one's artwork. More ropes, more knots, then untying one of them, while remaining in constant contact with him. That way, you get a smooth-flowing, enduring play session where there is little risk of getting boredom or cramps.

▼ Fashion

Looking good where it counts, not just on the runway. Why not turn up at the club on a Saturday night clad in an attractive bondage? Or to your Grandma's birthday party? Arriving at a bondage party already tied up has the added benefit of not having to carry around a rucksack full of ropes. And of course, the ties you advertise on your own body can be a calling card for all interested bottoms.

I'm not going to give instructions for entering the top league here, because—as you may have noticed—giving instructions for ropework isn't easy. And after all, I don't want you to be frustrated. But equipped with a few (basic) ideas, you can set off and explore on your own.

▶ Chest Harness

We'll start with an attractive chest harness. Take a long rope (15 meters would be great).

1. Place the bight around the back of your partner's (or your own) neck and let it hang loosely at the back. You'll need a bit of slack later on. If it's too tight, it will get uncomfortable very soon. And you've got a long night ahead of you. (This example demonstrates the benefits of marking long ropes in the middle).
2. Tie a double coin knot (see page 65) at the center of the sternum.
3. Do the same at the tip of the sternum (the little hollow just under your magnificent pecs) ...
4. And again at the navel and just above the pubic bone.
5. Then pull both ends back under your junk and, twisting them several times, draw them up over the back.
6. Pull the ends through the neck loop and then forwards under the arms towards the chest.
7. Thread each end through one loop in the top double coin knot.
8. Pull the ropes back.
9. Thread them through the twisted ropes ...

10 Then pull them forward and thread them through the next knot.

11 Back and through the twisted ropes, etc.

12 The upper body is now lusciously wrapped and ready for viewing.

13 The rear view ... good enough to eat!

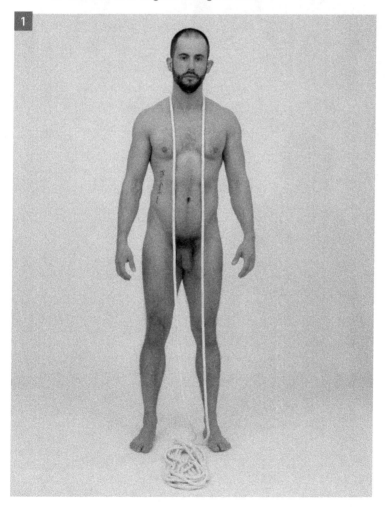

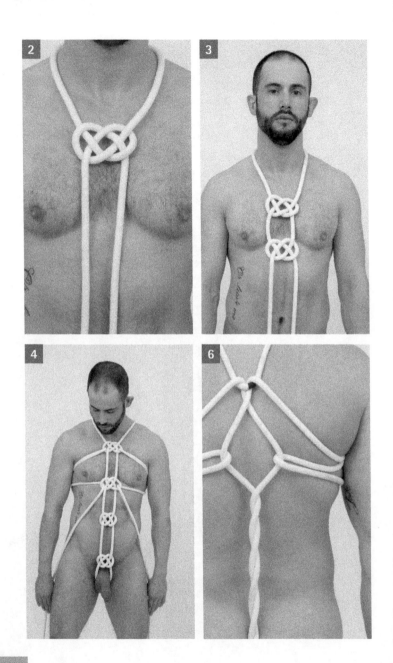

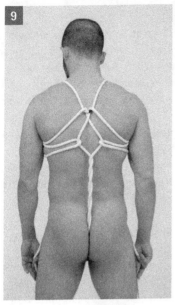

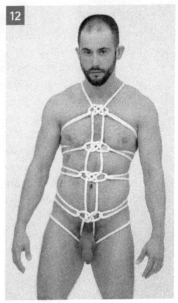

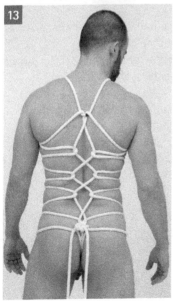

▶ Arm Binders

On the one hand, these are a great accessory to wear to fetish partys, on the other, you'll always have a rope "at hand" in case you need it, without having to carry it around in a bag or on your belt. For friends of hardcore fisting, these sorts of things can apparently also serve to enhance your enjoyment. But I couldn't possibly know firsthand.

As with all the ties described here, there are different ways of tying arm binders. This first variation may bring the stitches in knitting to mind, and may look a bit too artsy craftsy for some. But they have the unrefutable advantage of being easily untied like a run in a stocking.

For this binder we used a 7-meter rope.

1   Find the bight and place it on the forearm where you want the knots to be (they look best on the outer part, unless you want to hide them, in which case you should place it on the inside).
2   Then pass the double rope round under the arm, make a loop and pull this through the bight.
3   Now pass it around under the arm in the opposite direction, make a loop, and pull this through the last loop.
4   And so on and so forth.
5   Then just pull the ends through the last "stitch" (loop) ...
6   And secure them under and over the rope with a knot.
7   Finish off—as always—by pulling everything nice and tight so that it looks neat. After all, you want to make an impression.

Isn't that sexy?

Undo it by untying the final knot, pull hard, and the whole thing should fall apart.

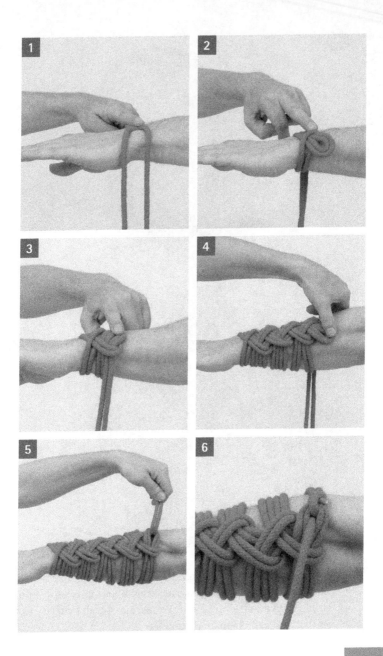

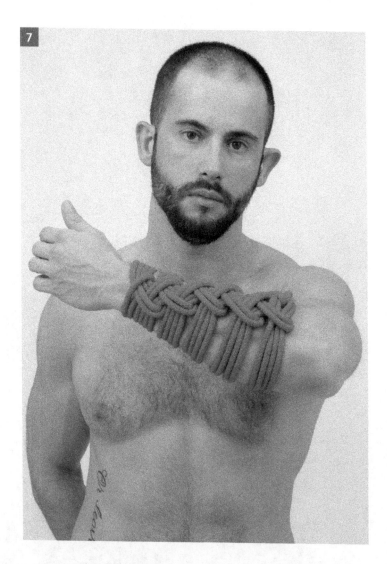

The second type of arm binder is just as simple. Personally, I think it looks nicer, but you can forget about untying it in a second. You've got to unpick it. We used a 7-meter rope here too, so that you can compare them.

1 Find the bight and pull the ends through to make an empty larks head. Pull this over your wrist.

2 Draw the rope over the top of your arm and hold it about 5 cm away from your hand ...

3 Then use the other hand to wrap it under your arm and pull it through under the top rope.

4 And once more: draw the rope up 5 cm, hold it, wrap it under your arm with the other hand, pull it through the top rope, etc.

5 Do not knot the rope at your elbow, the nerves are close to the surface there and it will hurt a lot!

6 Tie a knot when you've reached the top.

7 And again: Remember to pull it tight so that the ropes lie nice and flat.

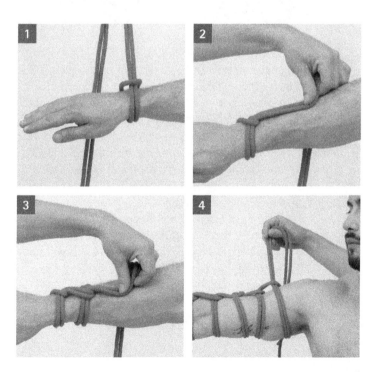

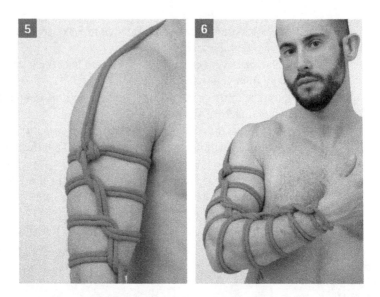

▶ Hangman's Noose

The hangman's noose can be considered the badge of bondage fans. But it's the same as with the red hanky worn around the neck: Not everyone who wears one is a fister. And just because someone doesn't wear one, it doesn't mean he isn't a fister (a triple negative, beat that). One way or another, it's a very nice fashion accessory. And in the immortal words of Patsy on *Absolutely Fabulous*: "You can never have too many accessories, darling."

1   Lay a piece of string on the table in front of you and make a loop in the middle. In order to better show you how it's done, we have made it not in the middle but to one side, so that one end is longer than the other. But if you want a decorative knot to wear around your neck, both ends should be the same length.

2   Now pull one part down and then up again, so that it looks a bit like a child's impression of a racetrack.

3 Then draw the lower part of the string over the other part.
4 And now wind it around ...

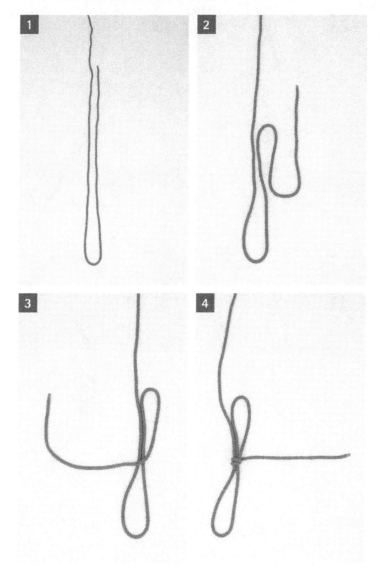

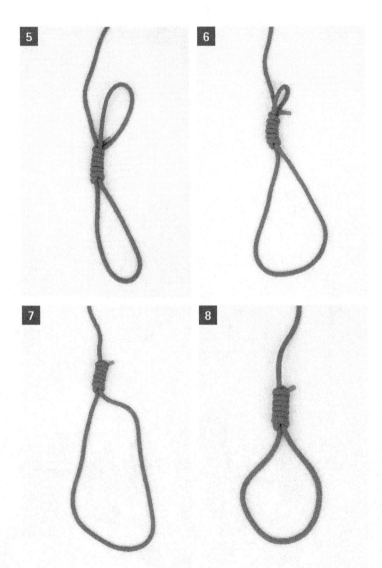

5   Over and over again, until the knot has reached the desired length.

6   Then pull the end you're winding with through the upper loop (in this case, you can only see a tiny bit poking out. If you want to wear it round your neck, you obviously need to make it longer).

7   Now draw in the upper loop by pulling on the lower loop until the upper one has disappeared into the knot and is secured.

8   You can shorten the noose by pulling the rope at the top, or lengthen it by pulling the noose.

Once you've tried this a few times with a piece of string, you can take a strip of black leather (in the thickness of your choice) and make the world's most exquisite hangman's noose. And if that doesn't attract the bondage freaks, at least you can shock the priest with it at your next confession!

Aftermath

Every game has its aftermath. So does bondage. The most important parts first: Never just unwrap the bottom and leave him there. If he has spent a longer period of time tied up, you should untie him slowly. Bondage often brings about an altered state of consciousness and you need to take your time to return, to recognize and reenter reality. Therefore I would advise you—if this is in keeping with the type of session—to release him "meditatively," with rest breaks and surprises, tenderly and sensuously, instead of tearing the ropes off him as if he were a gift you'd been waiting for. The bottom needs time to find his way back into his own outlines.

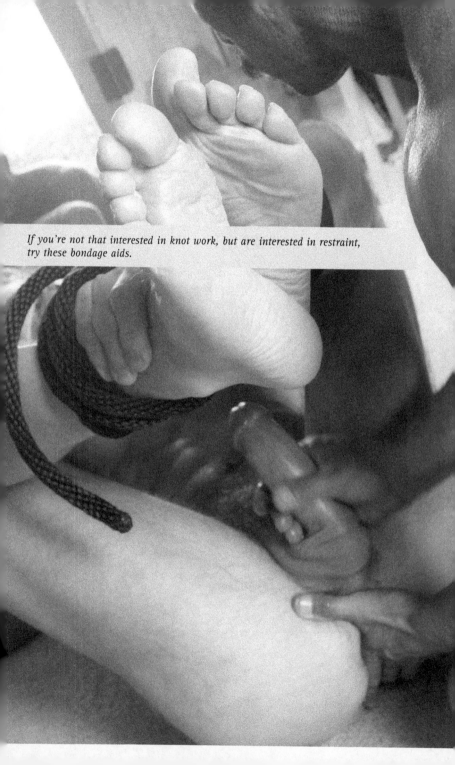

If you're not that interested in knot work, but are interested in restraint, try these bondage aids.

Aids for Quickies

If you don't want to spend hours tying knots, you can always fall back on a number of ready-made bondage products. These save time and might even fill a kinky need.

Bondage as a sex practice does not necessarily mean tying elaborate ropework on a person's body. If you prefer to concentrate on the person being tied, or being tied up yourself, you might want to start out with professional equipment specially designed for bondage. This applies especially to suspensions, which are less easy to learn.

By now, there are a number of great aids available to help you achieve a life in captivity, simply and quickly. I have put together a small selection here.

▼ Cuffs
There are many different models. Available in various sizes (as you need thicker ones for your thighs than for your wrists), they are also adjustable. Strapped to the joints like a belt around the waist, you can use the attached D-rings to secure your partner to, for example, a bed. The more elaborate models are padded on the inside—or with double straps for increased stability. Also available in rubber!

▼ Sleep Sacks

Imagine an object actually shaped like a sleeping bag, only tighter (so that the bottom can barely move, or preferably not at all) and which can be closed snugly around the neck (so that he can't get out by himself). Which brings us to our first problem: people come in all shapes and sizes ... There are a number of rings attached to the outside of the sleep sack (alternatively listed online under *body bag*), from which the entire thing can be suspended.

The more elaborate models can be adjusted to body size using all kinds of straps and buckles, so that your victim can be secured tightly. Zippers placed at strategic points facilitate access to your living plaything.

If someone puts you into a leather version of these things, this is serious business, as they can be quite expensive. Synthetic leather is generally used (and is easier to clean). Rubber etc is less durable and therefore unsuited to suspensions, but if can be quite nice to just lie on the floor. PS: Neoprene creates a similarly enjoyable sensation on your skin.

In case someone decides to stick you into one of these things, make sure he stuffs paper towels or rolled up bath towels in between your ankles and knees. Once you're in there tightly—and possibly gagged—you won't be able to tell him that the pressure of your bones on each other hurts like hell.

▼ Monogloves

These bondage aids, typically made of leather, enclose both arms in parallel and are tied behind the back. Some resemble large gloves, others consist of a leather strip running along the spine with a number of arm straps attached.

▼ Straitjacket

Well, I think we all have an idea of what that is. It's a jacket whose sleeves can be tied around the body with the aid of attached straps, so that the "patient" is unable to move. To prevent the restrained person from pulling the jacket over their heads, many straitjackets also feature a so-called crotch-strap which is pulled back through the legs and fastened at the back, as are the other straps.

Compared with other bondage techniques, straitjacket restraint may seem relatively comfortable at first. It should fit properly to prevent the straitjacketed person from escaping. This can be achieved by choosing the right size for the person wearing it. If the jacket is too small, it will restrict breathing, causing both physical and psychological damage.

If it's too large, it will be easier for the person wearing it to free their arms. Here too, the arms lie bent across the body, which can become quite painful after a time, due to the position and the impossibility of straightening the arms out. Again, the choosing the right size can be a decisive factor in comfort. Depending on what material is used, it can get very warm under a straitjacket–the restrained person will soon start to sweat profusely.

Playing with it is similar to the sleep sack, only with more leg room. And all the things you can do with it ...?!

And for those who like their sex with a spot of entertainment, you can relate the history of the straitjacket: invented in the 19th century by the "father of American psychiatry," Dr. Benjamin Rush, for use in, well, insane asylums. Their use has since been outlawed.

▼ Pillories

Yep, just like the middle ages. Once the bottom's head and hands are secured, the top is free to ravish the rest of his body. And what can you do with it ...? But as you see, as far as bondage is concerned, it is rather limited.

▼ Cock Cuffs

These funny looking things are designed to make getting an erection impossible, difficult or painful. Furnished with a lock, they deliver up the slave's pleasure to his master's whim. Great for mind control and pain play.

Cock cuffs are available in metal (hard and rough-edged) or leather. The more sophisticated models can be attached to harnesses or crotch ropes.

▼ Dog Collars

Just as cuffs are used to restrain the limbs, a collar can be used to attach the head somewhere. And that is—as I have probably already pointed out several times—the problem, or rather the danger. If the head is stuck somewhere, the body only has to slip and then it's a new commission for the undertaker. So, take care! Use a collar to take your slave for walkies, or keep him on a short leash, wear it as a fashion accessory or to signalize your preferences to others. But apart from that, the less experienced in particular should keep their necks out of it.

▼ Blindfolds

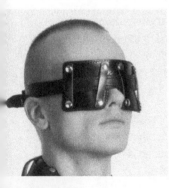

These should be familiar to anyone flying business class. Or from the windows of tacky sex shops, where you can get them in pink plush. But don't let that deter you. Restricting individual senses can increase your overall sensitivity during sex. In this case, blacking out your vision will heighten your sense of hearing and intensify your sense of smell.

PS: If you inhibit all of your facial senses, you focus on your own sensations. And that's not a bad thing.

▼ Gags

Gags can also be part of bondage. Ball gags, ring gags, bit gags, and penis gags, in every size and color, are popular—as are inflatable balloon gags. Alternatives to ready-made gags are also used, such as tape, pieces of clothing (smelly socks—mmm, lovely!—or old underpants) and scarves, or rather silk scarves. There are also masks with built-in gags.

▼ Masks

Instead of turning to gags, blindfolds, and earplugs, you can just use a mask to restrict all four senses (sight, hearing, taste and smell) at once. Zippers, gags and funnels allow for added stimulation to the poor wretch's head. There is a simply enormous variety. If you enjoy this type of sensual bondage, you should take some time and go and visit a well stocked store. You'll be surprised.

PS: With the aid of the attached loops and D-rings you can also use a mask to restrain someone's head.

▼ Bars

(Metal, bamboo or wooden) bars are always appropriate for spreading or tying things together or for adding some extra visual appeal to your work of art.

All hardware stores stock wooden or bamboo bars. Bamboo is lighter, plus its natural indentations prevent the ropes from slipping.

If you'd prefer a metal bar, you don't have to resort to some rusty iron bar you dug up out of the cellar or stole from the construction site next door. It might look good, but you'll ruin your carpets. Besides, it's incredibly heavy. Metal bars have one advantage over bamboo, in that professional spreader bars come with

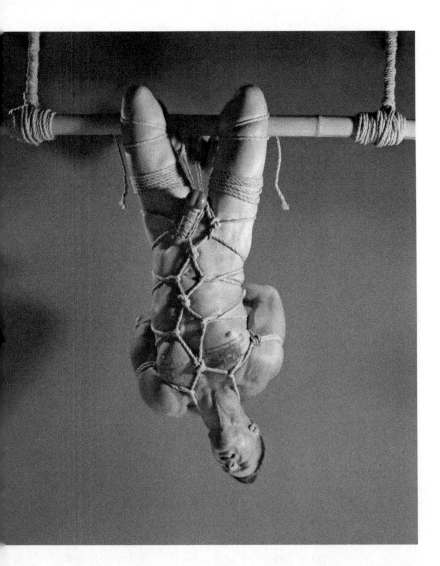

anchor points, which you can just hook your ropes onto and be ready in no time at all. There are also attachment points at the center to facilitate suspending the arms, for example, from a pulley or in a doorframe.

If you don't feel like spending a lot of money on a metal bar (I hope there are no retailers reading this!), try a shipping supplier. You can put together your own spreader bar out of parts designed for ships' rails, for a total cost of around 40 $. (A well-stocked hardware store, or, of course, the Internet will also have these parts.)

▼ Bars with Cuffs

If you really want to pull a fast one, just get a bar with pre-attached cuffs. Buckle up. And done! But as you can probably tell from the brevity of my description, this is no longer terribly relevant to bondage.

▼ Bondage Skirts

Not only does it look and feel great, fetishwear also works as bondage gear. Bondage skirts are the perfect example: These are skirts that fit your body tightly, so as to restrict movement.

The wearers of these skirts can only take teeny-tiny steps. Combined with high heels, this can equal total immobilization of the bottom, without any additional ties (kinky!!!). The materials of choice are (yet again) leather and rubber, although there are some tailors who use velvet, satin, or other materials.

▼ Bondage Suit

Not to be confused with the straitjacket. The difference is that the suit gives you a lot more freedom of movement. This tightly fitting suit also comes with all sorts of anchor points for physical restraints.

▼ Handcuffs

Well, there's not that much to say, except for: Pay attention to quality. You can give yourself a quite nasty injury with cheap cuffs. AND: Keep the keys somewhere sensible, especially if you're on your own, so that you can, at some point, enjoy your freedom once more.

▼ **Parachute or Safety Harness**

A second-hand parachute harness or safety harness used by rock climbers or construction workers can—if you can borrow one from somewhere—be a fun alternative. They are designed to let you sit in them halfway comfortably, and the padding reduces the risk of congestion and numbness. So you can find out if it's even your thing—without having to dig deep into your pockets.

▼ **Ceiling Hooks**

If you want venture on suspension bondage once you're a bit more experienced, you will definitely need a ceiling hook. One of those spiral-shaped things will do, the ones you use to hang up swings for children. The main thing is to fasten it to a ceiling joist to make sure it's secure. For concrete ceilings you'll need enormous toggle bolts (please consult a reliable builder).

Another alternative is to fasten a steel plate with a hook attached to the ceiling. Or else use an eye plate (boating supplies).

Before you suspend a living, breathing creature, please hang the corresponding weight from your hook for a while first (surely you have a few sandbags lying about?)!!!

▼ **Rings**

These rings, which look a bit like twisted Mercedes star symbols, are attached to the ceiling hooks. They enable you to thread your ropes through different loops and also make it easier to undo individual ropes.

▼ **Carabiner Connectors or Panic Hooks**

Panic hooks are snaps which, as opposed to carabiner connectors, can be opened easily, even under strong pressure. They are used in agriculture and expecially by riders as a safety measure, for example, when leading a horse. If the animal shies, you can open the panic hook and release him before anyone gets hurt.

Panic hooks are also used in BDSM. Especially in cases of the bottom fainting, the connection can be severed quickly and easily, even under heavy strain (i.e. his bodyweight). (Please do not undo the snaps while he is suspended upside down, or else he'll fall on his head!)

▼ Pulleys

The principle should be familiar to you from high-school physics. By (repeatedly) changing the direction of the rope, you can turn a mountain into a molehill. Particularly small and more delicate men will find it easier to hoist their partners up to lofty heights.

You can build your own pulley. But if you're going to suspend a human being from it, it's best to call in a professional. Well-stocked sex shops will be able to help you out.

▼ Suspensions

If you don't have a ceiling hook and just want to restrain your partner's hands above his head, you can easily tie your own suspension using a door ...

Simply tie two knots in a thick (8 -10 mm) rope, at the same distance as the width of the door. That gives you a loop on one side and two free ends on the other, depending on your requirements ...

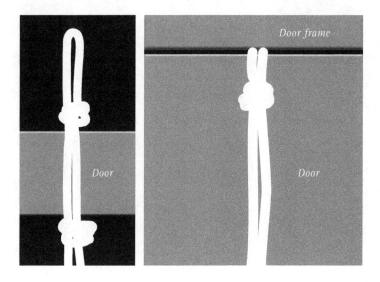

Bondage can be performed on fetish furniture to spice things up

▼ Cages

If your living circumstances (drywall ceilings) prevent you from creating a suspension, or if you simply can't put your trust in dowels and anchors, you can have a cage built for your bondage buddy.

▼ Furniture

Let your imagination run wild. All over the world, ingenious minds are designing exciting new furnishings that can be beautifully incorporated into bondage play.

Sales Assistance

If you are already familiar with a product (your favorite lube or condoms), you can go ahead and order it online. When buying fetish gear (aids and clothing) and definitely ropes, I strongly advise you to acquaint yourself with the products on the spot, by touching them, smelling them, and feeling them on your skin.

Especially when creating suspensions you should pay great attention to quality. A broken connector spells a crash landing for your bottom. For some pain freaks this may come as a welcome change, but most suspension fans will only suffer bruising and possibly even broken bones.

A real pro doesn't need a sling, just tons of ropes.

Want More Bang for Your Buck?

Now that you've mastered a few knots, you're ready to tie up all comers and head straight for the top. Slow down ... here's a brief look at what's in store for you.

For most people, the term bondage calls up the image of a man deliciously covered in ropes. But there are many other ways of restraining or immobilizing another person. I will illustrate some of these over the following pages. This chapter is called "advanced techniques" simply because all of these methods require a certain amount of experience. Not just ropework expereince, but also some knowledge of the body's functions and limitations, the vulnerability of the psyche, and the consequences that may result from improper handling. Wrapping someone up in aluminum foil may look like child's play at first glance. Which it is. Anyone can do it. But how long can someone be left like that? What will happen to him? What are the health risks?

As there are no blanket answers to these questions, always proceed slowly and with great care. Every new man is a new beginning. And always start out with simple techniques so that you can learn as you go, feeling your way towards confident handling.

Before we proceed to more sophisticated bondage techniques, we will begin with the long-awaited description of how suspensions work.

▼ Slings

How do you get a cow off the ice? You put it in a sling! This is perhaps the simplest way of creating a feeling of weightlessness. And—as long as the ceiling hooks are secure—it is quite safe, for a sling can hold an entire body, as opposed to ropes which only support a small area.

For a first taste of this feeling, just pay a visit to a well-equipped gay sauna (but take care, some people may assume that your spread legs are an invitation!).

While most slings are made of real or synthetic leather and chained to the ceiling, bondage artists prefer to rely on ropes and knots. This may be more time-consuming, but it's a lot more exciting than using a prefabricated sex swing.

▼ Suspensions

What's so hot about being hanging in mid-air? For one, it's the feeling of weightlessness. Your entire bodyweight suspended from a couple of ropes—this answer should satisfy the meditation, esoterics,

and campfire fans.

In an S-M context, suspending the bottom is mostly about taking away his stability. This can be incredibly unsettling. As long as you remain in contact with the ground, whether or not you're tied up, you're still in charge of the situation. As soon as you're hanging in mid-air, this arouses fears and anxieties which the top can take advantage of—and which the slave might well enjoy.

As with many things in life, the easiest-looking things are often the hardest. This is the case in any type of suspension. Now you might think it's incredibly difficult to raise a fully grown adult from the floor to a horizontal position, but that's the least of your problems. A much thornier topic is: safety. How to do it without injuring him? I'm referring not only to the dangers of falling, but also of straining and constricting body parts or even internal organs. Insufficient blood flow, contusions of the nerves, the muscles, the skin or the organs—these things are no laughing matter. The sinews and tendons can be subject to overstrain. An incorrectly balanced load can even cause dislocation of the joints. Remember, a fully-grown man equals a couple of hundred pounds of sheer body mass. With all this in mind, you might tie the knots too tightly and be unable to release the bottom in an emergency...

Not quite the "Hooray, I'm flying!" you envisioned, is it?

▼ How Do You Hang a Man?

"Not by the neck!"—your answer rings out like a shot. I cannot emphasize this enough.

The safest method is to hang the entire torso, by first knotting a good sturdy harness, distributing the weight over a number of ropes and then suspending your dreamboat from the ceiling by this harness as well as by several arm and leg ties.

You should be familiar with the harness and how it works from pages 104 to 106.

In contrast to ordinary bondage, you also have the suspension loads to reckon with. The ties should never tighten under strain!

Never tie suspension ropes around the abdomen. The only support the abdomen offers is soft tissue and a very fragile spine. Always tie around the chest and the limbs.

Please remember to support the head, otherwise you'll give the bottom a stiff neck at best. If the head bears down on the neck for too long, it can easily pinch a nerve.

Right, and another thing: suspensions are for short periods only. I don't mean a couple of hours, but rather a couple of minutes. Start out with two or three, allowing the bottom to enjoy it, then maybe five.

And: the smaller the area of contact between the rope and the body, the sooner you have to let him down.

▼ Where Do You Hang a Man?

Hang him from a sturdy hook in the ceiling, from a frame or from a door. For this, it is essential that your apartment (basement, garage ...) has either ceiling joists or a concrete ceiling. Modern buildings often have drywall ceilings, which might hold a lamp at best, but not a fully grown man!

If you're planning on suspending someone with lateral ties, remember to calculate the resulting shear stress, which causes the hooks to bend or the ropes to tear ...

▼ What Do You Hang a Man With?

For suspensions you will need sturdy, resilient ropes at least 6 mm thick. It is better to use even thicker ropes, for not only are they more resilient, they also provide a larger contact surface with the body and the pressure will be distributed more evenly.

▼ How Do You Hang a Man?

As explained above, it is best to use a harness as well additional ties around the shoulders, wrists, ankles, waist and thighs and then to raise the body horizontally with the aid of a pulley.

A traditional Japanese method is to tie the body up bit by bit and to suspend one body part after the next until he has lost contact with the ground entirely.

▼ Long-Term Bondage

Long-term bondage will evoke feelings of total helplessness, of being completely at someone's disposal, being continuously "used" and treated like an "object". The subject will feel he is absolutely defenseless and at the top's mercy, which can give rise to a profound feeling of submission.

The "loss of liberty" may also arouse intense feelings of being looked after, as all responsibility is handed over to the active partner.

Untying the bonds will create a feeling over (literal) release and

Breaking Strength

For those of you who won't let my warnings deter you:
Be aware of your rope's breaking strength! Don't use just any rope, don't use a stranger's rope, always use one you have bought yourself, where you know how much weight it will bear before it suddenly snaps and your bottom comes crashing down to the ground, breaking his ribs and his skull.

Always use ropes that will bear your body mass several times over without tearing.

Never suspend anyone from a single rope. Always use multiple ties, so that the other ropes will carry the load if one of the breaks.

Never put your trust in another man's rope!

a deeply felt need to be touched, which the top will then hopefully take full advantage of.

It is tempting to see long-term bondage as something you can do over the course of a week or more. As a general rule: If your bottom starts to go moldy, you've waited for too long.

Joking aside: even assuming you are the world's greatest tyer of knots, you haven't tied anything off, the bottom is in a stable position and has enough freedom of movement, it's still exhausting as hell. And of course you need to plan all the other little details. You can safely go without food for a while (unless the bottom has diabetes), but not without sufficient fluids. In order to be able to drink, the bottom has to be positioned accordingly (it's difficult to do head down): so keep a mug with a straw handy. And of course, fluids have to exit the body again at some point. Although...

Ropes are not necessarily the most suitable for long-term bondage, as no matter how you tie them, they will always constrict some body part or other. Moreover it can be quite uncomfortable (which is ok if you're doing S-M, but we're talking about long-term here ...) Sleep sacks are perfectly suited to these purposes. Beginners might

want to try it out with an ordinary sleeping bag. For the summer, or in a heated space, a thin cotton sleeping bag will do (or even a plain piece of linen). Let him get in and then wrap the whole thing up with duct tape, so that he can't escape.

I strongly advise against using steel (chains and handcuffs). This will cause chafing even over short periods of time. One sudden move and you're bleeding. And if that's not your kink ...

Hypothermia is another problem. If you lie without moving for a long time, your blood pressure will drop and you will get cold.

Of course, you must stay with the bound bottom for the entire period. If his limbs start to go numb, or become painful or swollen, you have to be able to release him immediately. He might have trouble breathing or start to panic. Be careful not to overtax him!

Oh well, there's one more point I should mention: However hot being at someone's mercy for a longer period of time may sound, however great it might "feel" in your imagination, in reality it can get dreadfully dull.

▼ S-M

Sadomasochism, pain play, dominance and submission, role play, this is a pretty broad field to cover and I would have to write a whole new (very large) book. But it should still be included in a bondage manual.

Bondage skills are an excellent requirement for taking away a bottom's defenses and leaving him at your mercy. After all, while you can make the ropework a humiliating experience in itself, it is also easier to whip a gagged subject, to piss on him and deliver him up to public derision. Nor will he be able to defend himself against a gang bang. Let the following illustrations inspire you.

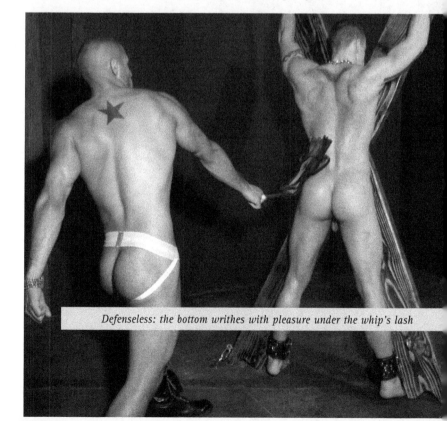

Defenseless: the bottom writhes with pleasure under the whip's lash

Breath Control

Breath control play is one of the most dangerous BDSM practices, as it restricts or even cuts off the bottom's breathing. The goal is to further incapacitate the bottom (once he has been deprived of his freedom of movement) by restricting his last independent bodily functions. Another effect of inhibiting breathing is that the blood builds up an oxygen deficit, the carbon dioxide levels increase and adrenaline is released.

This effect can be achieved quite easily by holding the bottom's mouth and nose closed. This is the best way of keeping an eye on him. Other methods involve using gas-masks, damp cloths, or chamois leather. The concept of *waterboarding* may also be familiar to you from the news.

This insert is just to inform you of the possibilities of this technique. If you are interested, seek an experienced practitioner. Breath control play is FUCKING DANGEROUS!!!

▼ Mummification

The most complete way of restraining someone is to render the bottom entirely motionless. The "easiest" way of doing this is with plastic wrap. To prevent him from escaping, start off by wrapping his arms and legs individually, followed by his body and then secure his arms to his sides and tie his feet together. Use rolled-up towels stuffed between his knees and ankles to protect them from too much pressure.

The whole thing is easiest to do standing up. If the bottom doesn't have the best sense of balance, you can first wrap his upper body while standing up and then help him lie down and raise his legs in the air at a 90° angle so that you can take care of them. However, there will be a bit left out around the midriff which will make itself unpleasantly felt as a difference in temperature.

You should never wrap the head itself, the mouth at least should remain free so that he can get enough air.

The advantage of using plastic wrap is that you can (carefully) cut or tear holes in it beforehand, so that you can ... ummm, access important parts.

When dealing with a recalcitrant bottom, you can, of course, reinforce your wrapping with strong tape. I wouldn't advise the use of gags with these kinds of extreme sports, so as not to hinder communication. After all, he has to be able to let you know if he doesn't feel well. Once he's fainted, it's already too late ...

And there's another thing you need to remember: plastic wrap—depending on how thickly it's wrapped—will make you sweat like a pig. But your body can't lose heat. So be especially vigilant and make sure your bottom doesn't overheat and pass out. Additionally, you should have a warm blanket at hand for when he emerges from his cocoon.

Releasing him is comparatively simple: Cut it open. Bandage scissors are best, as they have a blunt tip at the end, so that you don't cut his skin.

Last but not least: Always keep an eye on your bottom. He might secretly pass out and you won't notice unless you keep watching him.

▼ Plaster Bandages

Alternatively, try using plaster bandages—and do justice to the term mummification. As they have to be wet first, there is the added benefit of feeling the cold moisture gradually drying on your skin. It's a tingly feeling.

There are a number of disadvantages:

- It's sticky and messy. To avoid having to completely renovate your bedroom afterwards, you might want to lay down a pond liner first.
- Wrapping plaster bandages around a body is easiest with the "patient" standing up. This can however get a bit wobbly, especially when tying his legs together.
- It takes a while for the stuff to dry.
- Cutting holes (for example, in order to be able to reach the organs you might need for sex play) is not the easiest of undertakings.
- And releasing him at the end takes a while too.

▼ Vacuum Bed

For an all-encompassing feeling of restraint, the body bag or vacuum bed is often used. These are constructed along the lines of a full-body sleeping bag, from which, after the bottom has got in, the air is sucked out. The extremely low pressure (a vacuum isn't feasible) ensures that the enclosed body is very tightly sealed in and completely unable to move. As a rule, it is impossible to move even the fingers.

As a side effect, the senses can no longer fulfill their function. If

> **Blind Top**
> A fun idea for advanced players is to have the blindfolded
> top tie up the bottom. Of course, you will have to omit
> more complex bondages or suspensions, but the top's
> "blindness" means that he will have to find his way by
> touch. This can be a very sensual experience, provided you
> are really adept at the knots and can tie them blindfolded.

the ears are stymied by the noise made by the pump (for example, a
vacuum cleaner), this heightens the sensations on your skin.

There remains the question of how to breathe. Not an insignificant
question. Breathing is only possible through a tube leading outside—
a downright invitation to breath control play.

PS: I wouldn't let just anybody seal me in like that, certainly not a
complete stranger!

As these vacuum beds are generally made of latex or rubber, this
can be an added bonus to their kink appeal, especially for fetishists.

▼ Duct Tape

This truly unusual method should by no means be used during
longer play sessions. You place a chair or a stool in front of a
smooth wall and have the bottom stand on it. He stretches his
arms out to both sides, drooping slightly, with his legs spread out
as far as possible.

Now you use long strips to duct tape to gradually tape him to the
wall. Once you've secured him, slowly pull the chair (or stool) out
from under him. And your artwork is done.

There are at least three problems that may arise:

- A heat buildup under the tape (see *Mummification*). The only
  way of counteracting this is by not taping his entire body. Fin-
  ding the right balance between total taping for stability and
  partial taping for the sake of letting him sweat is a real achie-
  vement.

- Not using enough tape, using old tape or an unsuitable wall may cause him to fall off.
- Few people will enjoy this sticky feeling all over their naked skin. But wearing clothes doesn't make much sense either, as they rarely fit closely enough to ensure nothing slips. The only way to prevent it is by wrapping the entire body up in plastic wrap.

Oh, and I've just thought of something else: Make especially sure that his lower body has enough support. Too much weight on the arms will cause congestion.

▼ Mental Bondage

At a sex party in Vienna a few years back, I once stumbled over a Texan. I did actually stumble over him. But as there were men lying around everywhere, the only reason he caught my eye was because he had bootprints tattooed all over his body, as if someone had just stomped all over him wearing extremely dirty boots. Later on, he taught me about mental bondage.

As the name suggests, mental bondage dispenses with equipment. The only tie is the order given by the top to stay in a certain position. The bottom will then parry, feel tied, behave as if were actually tied, without a single knot. Except for the knot inside him, the mental tie.

A mental captive will immerse himself in the idea of being restrained. The most powerful stimulus in bondage takes place in the mind, so that the actual restraint is of no importance to mental bondage, which is centered solely around the mere idea of being tied and helpless.

At the same time, mental bondage is also an exercise in obedience. Depending on the position, holding it for any length of time will become very strenuous and uncomfortable sooner or later.

The positions the top chooses for the bottom can therefore either be purely functional or else represent a challenge for the bottom. After all, most players enjoy being the tiniest bit nasty now and again.

In order to test his obedience, the bottom is ordered to hold out his hands and a coin is inserted in between every two fingers. If he drops one of them, he will be punished.

As you see, this is power play more than anything else. Bondage freaks who enjoy being held by ropes won't appreciate it. And it's not an easy game to play, it can be a real challenge for a top. If you are only the slightest bit unconvincing, you will soon feel totally ridiculous.

▼ Being in Public

I'm very much afraid it'll be a long time before we are blessed with the sight of a gorgeous man tied up between the columns of Berlin's Brandenburg Gate. But for a bottom, the appeal of playing in public does not necessarily lie in actually being seen, but rather in running the *risk* of being seen. This feeling combines incredible humiliation and—depending on your psychological makeup—possibly pride at

Where am I? What's happening to me? Who can see me? Public bondage has its own special charm.

showing yourself. It may be a dare, it may be narcissism or exhibitionist tendencies.

Being in public does not necessarily entail being in a highly frequented place. Tying him up in a spread-eagle under a glass dining table (see page 113) and inviting a few friends over for coffee is no less humiliating to a bottom. Depending on his purpose, they could either ignore him or use him. A blindfold adds extra appeal, as he won't even be able to tell who the guests are (Grandma, the boss, the neighbors?), or what is going on around him.

It can also be enough to tie your slave up in the living room and then just pretend to invite people over. Making a phone call and alluding to an invitation can create an incredible buildup of anticipation ... there are no limits to your imagination. However, you should always make sure that your own fantasies run along the same lines as those of your bottom. Overstep your boundaries, expose him to ridicule, abuse him in any way, and you can be sure he will never ever invite you to another Grand Prix party.

▼ Couples Bondage

Couples bondage is actually a game that can definitely be played by beginners as well. I have listed it under advanced techniques because in my experience beginners tend to be so absorbed in the knots that they aren't really in the mood to play. On the other hand, it might be a good idea to lie down on the floor with your partner and a couple of ropes and to see what happens once you start playing with them.

One person ties a rope around the other's ankle and pulls it over his shoulder. The other fastens his rope to his partner's cock and holds the other end in his mouth, pulling at it gently. Both of them move around each other, entwined in one another, pulling each other towards them with the ropes, etc.

During the course of the game, you can certainly make sure your partner's mouth just so happens to land on your own hard dick, or his cock ends up in your ass. Part of this game's attraction is to become entangled with one another and to discover who leads whom, who looks after himself, who gets what he wants ... and who doesn't—without ruling out any resulting drama in your relationship.

Together means more. Tie your partner into the game and rediscover yourself.

This game has the advantage of there being no right and wrong. You can use everything that happens to one another's benefit. And unless you bungle it up completely, you probably won't manage to injure each other. Have fun!

Together means more. Tie your partner into the game and rediscover yourself.

Advanced Games Are Only for the Experienced!

Some of the techniques listed here seem pretty tame, but trust me when I list them under the heading "only for the experienced." Find yourself a trustworthy practitioner with years of experience and try out the techniques described here on your own body before you take on the responsibility of subjecting another person to these sensations. That way, you won't overtax other people and you'll protect yourself. You wouldn't believe how easy it is to overexert oneself.

Keep your scissors at hand, but make sure no one hurts themselves with them.

Safety First

In my experience, bondage is the most accident-prone sexual practice there is. Simply because ropes can lead an upredictable life of their own.

The sheer length of the list of do's and don'ts may give rise to dismay. But a little dismay can't hurt. Rope play is dangerous. Many people have been injured doing it, some have even died.

But don't worry, many of the rules are just common sense. I have listed them here anyway, because during sex, especially when things get really hot, common sense is often left far behind and there isn't really much left to rely on. Especially not your head–after all, for many people the main point of sex is to forget themselves.

▼ Creating a General Framework for Rope Play

One essential condition for satisfying rope play is mutual trust. As the person being tied up is at the mercy of the active person, he has to be able to depend unconditionally on the agreed boundaries and on the effectiveness of the safe word.

One the other hand, the top has to be able to rely on the bottom's ability to gauge his own limitations, especially those concerning his physical and mental well-being. This negotiation, in which desires, boundaries and fantasies are communicated, takes place before the session and is a key safety component.

Simple safety measures include having a pair of bandage scissors ready, keeping spare keys to locks and handcuffs in a safe place, and avoiding knots around the neck and the joints to rule out fainting and permanent nerve damage.

Many especially impressive scenes depicted in bondage photos and videos have been staged by experts, known as riggers, and should not be imitated by anyone without an acute grasp of the techniques, a fundamental knowledge of anatomy and physics and a corresponding wealth of experience. This is especially relevant within those grey areas between bondage and BDSM that play with the bound person's fears or use breath control. There are also many extremely artistic Japanese bondages that can only be accomplished without endangering the bottom—or at least kept at a low risk level—if one has years of experience and has reached a very high level of expertise beforehand.

When You Assume, You Make an Ass out of U and Me.

"Never assume anything, check everything!" If you really take this rule to heart, you will always be on the safe side. To show you what I mean by "assume," here are a few suggestions:

- Never assume a rope will hold just because it looks as if it will.
- Never assume a ceiling hook will hold just because you were promised it would.
- Never assume your bottom is telling the truth when he says he can stand anything.
- Never assume he is telling the truth when he says he is psychologically sound.
- Never assume he's not on drugs.
- Never assume he will be delighted at being tied up.
- Never assume he wants to lose control.
- Never assume he's trustworthy just because of his beautiful blue eyes.
- Never assume he will intuitively know where your boundaries are and respect them.
- *Never assume anything, check everything!* Articulate your expectations and limits and make sure that your partner has understood you correctly. If you're not sure, get out of there!

▼ An Overview of the Rules

- Do not trust a complete stranger.
- Discuss your boundaries with your partner and make sure you have an understanding.
- Find out about your partner's health issues. No matter whether you tie him up or he ties you up, once one of you is "on the ropes," it's already too late. These include: accidents, back or neck injuries, or operations? Problems with circulation? Trouble breathing? Asthma, panic attacks? Fainting? Arrhythmia? And increasingly: silicone implants? (Yes, those are a thing. Really.)
- No rope play if there are drugs involved, if one of you is overtired, or suffering from severe emotional stress.
- Even if it's a game, take bondage seriously!
- Agree on an unmistakable stop code. If begging and pleading are part of the game, then "No, please, no!" is not going to work. Rather choose something that has nothing to do with sex. Traffic lights—green, amber, red—have proven reliable.
- If you're using a gag, have the bound person hold coins in his hand. Dropping them means "Stop!" (Of course, this won't work with loud music or thick carpeting.)
- Never use utensils you are not familiar with.
- Never load a rope over and above its quality. Broken ropes go straight in the trash!
- Never overtax your partner, neither the top nor the bottom.
- Always have a pair of scissors at hand. And I don't mean nail scissors. They have to be able to quickly cut through the thickest of ropes.
- If you're using locks, keep a spare key at hand.
- No intentional or unintentional breath control play!
- Never tie the neck into your ropework!
- Stay in constant contact with your partner during bondage. This is the only way you can be sure that he is conscious, that his breathing is not restricted and that your ties aren't cutting off his circulation.
- Never leave a tied up person alone.
- Don't spend too much time, this can cause overexertion.
- If anything goes wrong, rule number one is: Stay calm! (I know, it's easy enough to say.)

What to Do in Case of an Emergency

If he passes out, lay him on his back and remove all the ties straight away. Take him out of the danger zone, meaning: find a quiet corner in the darkroom or the club. Raise his legs so that the blood can flow back and make sure there's fresh air. If he doesn't come round right away, call emergency services (911 nationwide). If he is unconscious but breathing, put him in the recovery position. If he isn't breathing, now is the time to test your knowledge of resuscitation measures ...

Photo credits

	page
TomBianchi.com:	30, 51, 166, 196
BoundJocks.com:	12, 20, 40, 123, 124, 128, 134, 142
butcherei.com:	169, 170 bottom
RickCastro.com:	24, 26, 108, 119, 138, 147, 176, 187
Channel1Releasing.com:	103
FalconStudios.com:	17, 18 top, 112, 117, 120, 130, 180, 185, 186, 194, 199
iStock.com/gerenme:	14
iStock.com/nikitje:	54
Mischa Gawronski:	16 top, 60, 66, 68, 69 top, 70, 71, 72, 73, 75, 76, 77, 79, 80, 81, 82, 83, 87, 88, 89, 90, 91, 92, 94, 95, 96, 98, 104, 105, 106, 110, 111, 113, 114, 115, 116, 122, 125, 126, 127, 132, 135, 136, 137, 139, 140, 141, 143, 144, 145, 146, 148, 150, 151, 152, 155, 156, 157, 159, 160, 161, 162, 163, 164
HotHouse.com:	10/11, 171 top, 191
Steffen Kawelke:	32, 37, 61, 62, 63, 64, 65, 67,175
LucasEntertainment.com:	100
Misterb.com:	16 bottom, 167, 170 top, 170 center, 171 center, 173
Stephan Niederwieser:	43, 45, 47, 49, 53, 55
VanDarkholme.com:	13, 14 bottom, 15, 19, 25, 42, 56, 58, 69 bottom, 78, 118, 172, 178, 184, 192, 201

Thanks to:

Everything a Man Needs to Know

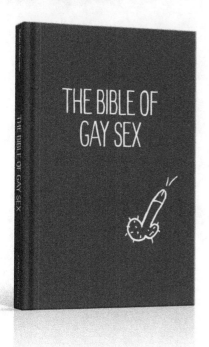

Stephan Niederwieser
THE BIBLE OF GAY SEX
256 pages, softcover,
17 x 24 cm, 6¾ x 9½ "
ISBN 978-3-86787-447-2
US$ 32.99 / € 24,95

Hallelujah! Finally there is a book that tells you ALL you need to know about gay sex. For let's be honest: Talking sex is only easy as long as you can play the part of the experienced lover.

Stephan Niederwieser—author of various sex guides—informs you about everything you need to know, whether it's dating, health, the best ways to relax or the responsible use of stimulants. *The Bible of Gay Sex* is richly illustrated; it's a competent and entertaining book about everyone's favorite pastime.

MrB

LEATHER RUBBER TOYS

AMSTERDAM
WARMOESSTRAAT 89

BERLIN
MOTZSTRASSE 22

PARIS
24 RUE DU TEMPLE

24/7
MISTERB.COM

FACEBOOK.COM/MRB.AMSTERDAM